Hope. Healing. Pain. Fear. Doubt. Victory. In *Battles and Breakthroughs:
Setting Captives Free,* Joel and Stephanie Midthun share their real-life journey
of healing that comes in the Father's love. This is no simple story of a veneer
of healing. This is a deep and penetrating account of how Jesus moves in his
love and grace into the deeper waters of our life experiences to bring forth life
and peace from pain and wounds. Please enter into the story and experience
healing for you and those you love.

— DR. JOHN JACKSON, PRESIDENT OF WILLIAM JESSUP UNIVERSITY
(JESSUP.EDU), AND SPEAKER AND AUTHOR ON
LEADERSHIP AND TRANSFORMATION

The message that Pastor Joel and Stephanie Midthun share is one that has
impacted our pastors and leaders here in Tanzania in a powerful way. Their
vision and message challenges us leaders to be a part of bringing freedom for
those who are captive—especially victims of human trafficking. But it's also
a message that challenges and inspires us leaders to be healthy and whole as
we serve others in our communities. I highly recommend the book *Battles and
Breakthroughs* and know it will be a very practical resource for the leaders of
our churches.

— PASTOR ELINGAYA SARIA, ASSISTANT BISHOP OF THE
EVANGELICAL LUTHERAN CHURCH OF TANZANIA, NORTHERN DIOCESE

Battles and Breakthroughs is a true and honest account of setting the captives
free. If you're expecting just a manual of spiritual warfare, this isn't it. It's much
more than that. It is a book of raw honesty and great depth with outstanding
practical help regarding the wholeness and all-around health of the believer.
The authors talk about their personal journeys pre-ministry and, more-so, the
challenges faced whilst in ministry. Each chapter can be used as a reference for
a particular aspect of their insight into freedom and subsequent wholeness. We
highly recommend this book to all believers!

— PASTORS JOHN AND DEBBIE BULLOCK, FOUNDERS AND
DIRECTORS OF SOUL CAMP, AUTHORS OF INTO AFRICA FOUNDATION,
THE GATEHOUSE INTERNATIONAL CHURCH, MOSHI, TANZANIA

While reading Stephanie and Joel's kingdom adventures, I feel like I am sitting in a room with two dear friends who love me and are inviting me into their lives, hearts wide open to me. Jesus is present with me in their story. I am not alone. They are cheering me on to find my voice and hear the sound of the song Jesus is singing over me. I feel compelled to run at least one leg of the race with Joel and Stephanie that God has set before them, fixing our eyes on Jesus, who for the joy set before him endured the cross, scorning its shame...who now enables us to not grow weary and lose heart (Hebrews 12:1–3). I bless each one of you who reads this book with the gift of freedom through the power of the Holy Spirit to be who God created and called you to be.

— DR. JOE JOHNSON, Pastor and Director
of Heart of the Father Ministries

This is, hands down, one of the best and most powerful books I've ever read in my life. I highly recommend it to people. The fact that the authors speak out against child trafficking and God's calling upon their lives says volumes about their level of self-awareness, and this book builds on that. That it is also written by both husband and wife shows what happens when a marriage is built on a strong foundation. They get it. They've been there. They have an answer that gives hope and produces results. They have experiences to back up what they say, and that is priceless.

— EDNA SIMBI, Department of Social Welfare,
California, Awarded the 2016 U.N. Change Maker's
Award, Courage Worldwide Board Member

Joel and Stephanie Midthun have written a book of hope! In *Battles and Breakthroughs in Setting Captives Free*, they transparently share how they were betrayed, wounded, disappointed, perplexed, assaulted, rejected, and slandered...to name just a few of their experiences. But theirs is no cry for pity. They write how their cries of pain have been transformed into songs of deliverance as God uses their "sacred wounds" to propel them into ministry to others, including those who have been orphaned and trafficked sexually. Their lessons of hope, healing, and victory inspire all of us who have had similar experiences. The questions and exercises at the end of each chapter were helpful too. Read this book and be transformed to help others!

— DENISE SIEMENS, Founder of Arise!
Women and ElevateHER ministries

Battles and Breakthroughs in Setting Captives Free is captivating, deeply personal, and vulnerable. Jesus was a storyteller and so are Joel and Stephanie Midthun. They, too, teach with living examples—stories of assault and miracles and breakthrough. Some are heart-wrenching, of children robbed of their soul and dignity through human trafficking. Accounts of real people bring the biblical reality of demonic oppression into focus. The testimonies tell us about promise and persecution. Throughout the book, we get some good teaching, like the importance of emotional health. They found that out like we all need to—the personal way, by seeing their own brokenness and need for God to heal their past to give them a rich future, all of which finds its way into this lively, upbeat book. Their "brave, new world" is now Tanzania, Africa, though Joel grew up in Africa as a missionary kid. They give oversight to Courage House—helping children, youth, and adults find freedom from tyranny. What a wonderful story. I'm sure you'll enjoy it too!

— REVEREND PAUL ANDERSON
AUTHOR, SPEAKER, AND RENEWAL LEADER

Battles
&
Breakthroughs

In Setting Captives Free

JOEL & STEPHANIE MIDTHUN

Battles & Breakthroughs in Setting Captives Free

© 2018 by Joel & Stephanie Midthun

COPYEDITED BY:
Jennifer Edwards
jedwardsediting.net

BOOK DESIGN BY:
Linné Garrett
829 DESIGN
829Design.com

COVER DESIGN BY:
Mitchell McCleary

ISBN: 978-1-7202326-3-6 Paperback

Available at Amazon.com

Printed in the United States of America

✣ DEDICATION ✣

This book is dedicated to our beloved family;
our parents who live(d) and love(d) so very well;
daily praying for us and modeling a life of bold faith, quiet surrender,
deep commitment for better or worse, humble generosity, and radical
obedience—even to the ends of the earth!

And to our three precious sons—
you bring us so much joy and laughter.

We love watching you chase after your dreams.

✤ CONTENTS ✤

✛ FOREWORD ✛

LIFE AND MINISTRY ARE FILLED WITH BATTLES AND WITH BREAKTHROUGHS. Learning to navigate that journey well is essential to both our health and wholeness as persons and our effectiveness as leaders in the kingdom of God. Stephanie and Joel Midthun are two people who have learned to navigate that journey of life and ministry well.

Battles and Breakthroughs in Setting Captives Free is a book about experiencing God's love and grace, and his transforming work in and through our own battles and breakthroughs. As Director for the Alliance of Renewal Churches (ARC), I work with pastors and lay leaders in the United States and overseas. Rarely have I found anyone who has the integrity between their vision and passion and how they actually live their lives; I have found this in Stephanie and Joel Midthun. Steph and Joel have experienced the message of this book, they are living the message of this book, and they are equipping others to carry out the ministry of Jesus to set captives free.

Not only are Stephanie and Joel involved in ministries that set captives free and equip others to participate in that kind of ministry, they are doing it from a place of emotional, relational, and spiritual wholeness. Their example in this regard is a living model to all who serve as leaders in the body of Christ. Too many leaders have significant wholeness deficits in their lives, and as a result, they are held captive by things in their past that are still influencing their present in unhelpful ways. The very charisma of many leaders that we so often applaud can mask such deficits. Growth in wholeness is essential because what we do not allow God to transform, we will transmit. The truth is that the captives who often need to be set free are not just "others," but are in fact "us."

Battles and Breakthroughs in Setting Captives Free is a book well worth taking the time to read. I do not say this lightly. As one who has a busy ministry and personal schedule, I know how difficult it can be to build in time to read. But if you make the time to read this book, you will be encouraged and refreshed, and you will be further equipped to be someone through whom God can set people free. That kind of life is life worth living. That kind of life is the life Stephanie and Joel Midthun are living and now share with us in this book. Thank you, Joel and Steph!

— MIKE BRADLEY
Director of the Alliance of Renewal Churches (ARC)
Author of *Being a Safe Place for the Dangerous Kind*
Gilbert, Arizona

August 2018

✣ ACKNOWLEDGEMENTS ✣

TO ALL OF THE DEAR PASTORS AND LEADERS WHO HAVE BEEN so influential in our lives over the years; you have loved, preached, taught, counseled, believed, comforted, prayed, encouraged, corrected, supported, and challenged us. You have cheered us on and some of you are in heaven still cheering us on! Thank you Pastor Eric Hoefer, Pastor James Hoefer, Pastor Neil Watson, Don Gutzman, Cliff Pederson, Dr. Luverne Tengbom, Dr. Norman J. Lund, Pastor Chuck Carlson, Dr. Joe Johnson, Pastor Luthor Nelson, Pastor Jay Huckabone, Pastor Paul Anderson, Pastor Darrel Deuel, Pastor Mike Bradley, Denise Siemens, Dr. Gil Stieglitz, Dr. John Jackson, Pastor Rob Lane, Assistant Bishop Elinga Saria, Archbishop Frederick Shoo, Pastor Elisha Mahene, Pastor John Bullock, Jenny Williamson, Darla Calhoun, and my (Joel's) brothers Pastor Eric Midthun and Chaplain Erling Midthun. And to my (Stephanie's) sisters, Carolyn and Christy, thank you for sharing your beautiful songs and their powerful stories.

WE LOVE AND HONOR EACH ONE OF YOU FOR THE IMPACTFUL ROLE YOU PLAYED IN OUR LIVES.

✢ INTRODUCTION ✢

JESUS CAME TO "SET THE CAPTIVES FREE," AND AS BELIEVERS WHO FOLLOW HIM, it is our call to join him in this kingdom work. But often, we are captive to our own heavy chains and sometimes don't even know it. Tough seasons in life and the demands of ministry can do a lot of damage to our souls. Personally, we have found that there has been a high cost to our calling, especially since we have entered in the fight against human trafficking—specifically, sex trafficking of children.

The road for us in ministry has been both fulfilling and challenging. In fact, it has been brutal at times. The highs have been oh, so high, and the lows so very low; there have been twists and turns we could have never imagined. This is a deeply personal journey we are sharing with you, as we have recounted the seasons in our life and our many battles and breakthroughs— we admit, sometimes we needed to stop and shed a few tears. But then we would give thanks to God for all He has done in us through those times.

God has been so merciful to us, setting us free where our own hearts were held captive. And while we individually had very different journeys to wholeness, God brought us both to the same place of wanting nothing more than to see freedom and wholeness in our lives and the lives of others— from our own family, to children living on the streets in Africa, to victims of human trafficking around the world, to the congregations we served, as well as to pastors and missionaries.

True freedom is possible, but the storms come and battles wage over our lives and our destinies. Sometimes, it is an all-out war and many of us aren't prepared to fight it or survive it, yet alone thrive in it.

You see, we have found over the years that very few people walk in wholeness, even those leading ministries. There can be an emphasis on "holiness" more than "wholeness" in the church; in "gifts of the Spirit" more than "fruit of the Spirit;" in "spiritual growth" more than "emotional health."

How is it that people can sit in church week after week and see no transformation in their lives? There is also much burn out among pastors and leaders; many are just going through the motions or they just give up and quit.

We Almost Did

We are so grateful that God gave us families and healthy mentors who loved us, believed in us, corrected us, and poured into us when we needed it most. We found a safe place to heal from wounds, to grow in our faith and character, and to be challenged to live out our destiny with courage.

We don't claim to have all the answers, yet we've been given tools, revelations, and strategies from others, as well as through our own experiences that have helped us in many breakthroughs. These have equipped us and shown us what it really means to be free—to live a fulfilling life and help others do the same.

So now, we pay it forward and cheer others on!

To those who have been victimized and still carry that deep pain, to those in ministry who are weary of the battles and struggles and want to quit, or to those who simply want more tools for themselves and for others to stay strong and courageous in their call— whatever that may be,

... *this is for you.*

We now live in Tanzania, Africa, and "uhuru" means "freedom" in Swahili. True freedom is our heart's cry for us and for you. It is God's battle cry over us all, and He is singing this song of freedom over us.

Can you hear it?

I.

Setting Captives Free

FREEDOM

/fri:dem/ "the state of not being enslaved or imprisoned"

I, STEPHANIE, HAVE BEEN A WORSHIP LEADER FOR OVER THIRTY YEARS. WHEN I was in my early 20s, I had a dream that has stuck with me all these years. I was leading worship, and no matter how much I tried to encourage the church to worship God with freedom and joy, I looked out and the faces of the congregation looked depressed, discouraged, or unengaged. Most of us worship leaders have had this happen at times and, believe me when I say it is exhausting and no fun, to say the least! But in my dream the Lord spoke to me and said, "Look at their hands and their feet." I looked and suddenly saw heavy balls and thick iron chains on their ankles and around their wrists. It was impossible for these people to worship freely, because they were all in their own personal prisons, even though they were Christians and part of a good church. How could this be? Isaiah 61:1–3 proclaims,

> "The Spirit of the Sovereign Lord is on me, because the Lord has anointed me to preach good news to the poor;
>
> He has sent me to bind up the brokenhearted, to proclaim freedom for the captives and release from darkness for the prisoners;
>
> To proclaim the year of the Lord's favor (Jubilee) and the day of vengeance of our God; to comfort all who mourn,
>
> and provide for those who grieve in Zion—to bestow on them a crown of beauty instead of ashes, the oil of gladness

3

instead of mourning, and a garment of praise instead of a spirit of despair.

They will be called oaks of righteousness, a planting of the Lord, for the display of his splendor." (NIV, emphasis mine)

After his baptism in the wilderness for forty days and his temptation from the enemy, Jesus returned to Galilee in the power of the Spirit. Luke 4:18–19 records that he read from the prophet Isaiah and said,

"The Spirit of the Lord is on me, because he has anointed me to preach good news to the poor.

He has sent me to proclaim freedom for the prisoners and recovery of sight for the blind, to release the oppressed, to proclaim the year of the Lord's favor."

Then Jesus said something radical.

"Today this scripture is fulfilled in your hearing" (Luke 4:21).

This was shocking and outlandish to all who heard him. This was the very moment when Jesus began his public ministry. He was fulfilling this prophetic promise and proclaiming his holy purpose on the earth. He came for the poor, for the prisoners, for the blind, and for the oppressed. He came to proclaim the year of the Lord's favor, Jubilee, which historically was commanded to be celebrated every fifty years. This was the year after completing seven cycles of seven years (7x7=49), an extra-special year when all debts were canceled, all property that had been lost was restored, and all indentured slaves were given freedom. By Jesus proclaiming the fulfillment of Jubilee, he was speaking new life, new possibilities, and new freedom to his people, Israel—a people under the yoke of oppression, depression, and bondage; politically to the Roman Empire, spiritually to the legalism of the Pharisees, and emotionally to the years of exile and unfulfilled expectations.

So, if Jesus had a driving purpose to set the prisoner free, and we are his followers, shouldn't that be our purpose since we are to do *his* works?

"Truly, truly I say to you, whoever believes in Me, will also do the works that I do; and greater works than these will he do" (John 14:12).

Yes, Jesus wants to set us free so that we can bring freedom to others.

My Story

"Jesus came to set the captive free, but the enemy came to take the free captive." ~ Beth Moore

My name "Stephanie" means *crowned one* or *victorious one*, as in someone who has run a race and won, receiving the victor's crown.

I believe strongly that often our names hold a spiritual meaning and keys or clues for our destiny. My friend Jenny Williamson teaches this at her Courage Conferences, and it is amazing how accurate this truth has been for the women who come. And for me, the very destiny of my name is where the enemy has battled and fought to bring defeat in my life, trying to make me quit or even attempting to take me out of the race altogether.

I was baptized as a baby. Having been raised in the Lutheran church with an understanding of who God is, I did not fully grasp a personal relationship with Him. I learned the basics of the Christian faith and knew a few passages about the Bible, especially Psalm 23, which I remember my mom helping us to memorize when we were young. It was one of the few Scriptures I knew very well by heart. My dad and I had a bit of a strained relationship, even though he was very involved in our lives. He was a strict military father, an Air Force pilot and later a commercial pilot. I was a bit of a free spirit and found myself wanting to grow up way too fast. I looked much older than I was and craved the attention I got at much too young an age.

The summer before I turned thirteen, I went to South Dakota for several weeks to babysit my baby cousin while my aunt and uncle worked on their cattle ranch. I loved that special place where my mom grew up. The independence went to my head, though, and I decided to be grown up and wear lots of make-up and very short shorts. I gained some weight and got curvy. My parents were shocked when they came to pick me up, hardly recognizing me after only six weeks! Oh, the battles after that. I so wanted to be grown up, while my parents wanted me to look and act my age. Thus started a season of rebellion and a lot of tension in our home over the next few years.

I was barely thirteen when a popular boy who lived in our neighborhood took notice of me. He was a couple years older than me, and being insecure, I liked being noticed by him. He convinced me to sneak over to his house one night while our parents were sleeping, and I found myself in a situation beyond my control. Against my attempts to resist, I lost my innocence that night. Actually, it was stolen from me. I was traumatized, confused, and felt dirty, and was left with a very twisted view of love and sex. Sadly, after I went home that night, I whispered in my heart maybe he does love me, and tomorrow at school I will be his girlfriend for everyone to see. I wasn't quite prepared for the moment I saw him the next day, when he turned away and acted like he didn't even know me. My young tender heart was completely crushed. But my heart craved love, even if it was a distorted version of it. I was willing to settle, even if it meant feeling "loved" for just a few moments.

That night, I also lost something else—my voice. I realized it much later in life, but that was the first experience I had where I lost my ability and my confidence to say "no." Because of that, I lacked healthy boundaries throughout my teenage years and grew used to the feeling of being used. I was filled with a lot of self-hatred, although I had a lot of friends. I used to look in the mirror and say to myself, I hate you. I was rebellious, always breaking the rules at home. Being wild and having fun with my friends was my main goal in life, even if I knew I would be grounded for my bad choices.

During my teen years, our family became quite involved in church life, and I saw my dad changing as he grew in his faith. My parents eventually became leaders in our church, and my sisters and I were active in youth groups and choirs. I grew in my faith but was living a double life. I was president of our church youth group and professed to love Jesus but would often party with my school friends on weekends, drinking and sneaking out. The self-hatred continued to grow in my heart.

One night at sixteen years old, I impulsively decided I wanted it all to end. Overdosing on pills, I cried myself to sleep not knowing if I would live through the night. I woke up a couple of hours later hallucinating and seeing ugly creatures in my room, which were probably a combination of demons and the toxicity of the drugs. I was terrified and lonely and cried out to Jesus to save my life. I prayed out loud sobbing and said, "I don't really want to die, Jesus!" Immediately, I vomited several times and then slept. When I woke up in the morning, I was grateful and so relieved to be alive. My ears were ringing from the effects of taking all those pills, but other than that, I seemed to be physically okay. My mom was on the couch, and I curled up next to her and put my head in her lap. I vowed in my heart that I wouldn't tell anyone what I had done. I had to read people's lips when they talked to me for the next couple of days because the ringing in my ears was so loud. A new reality began to set in, though—maybe, just maybe—God spared my life because He had a purpose for me.

Later, my parents discovered what I had done, and in consulting with a doctor, he said that at the very least I should have had organ damage, or I should have died. God truly did hear my cry. My dad and I had a conversation that I will never forget. He said he saw me living on both sides of the fence with my faith and that it was time I made a choice. Would I follow Jesus or would I go my own way and follow the enemy? It was another defining moment, and I committed my life wholeheartedly to Jesus later that night when I went to bed. I knew God was real, that He had spared my life; I also knew that I wanted to follow His ways and know Him more.

I loved our youth group and our youth pastor, James Hoefer. It was a sweet time of growing in our faith as a family. Pastor James saw some deep insecurities and struggles in me when I was interviewing for a summer job to work with kids at our church, and he asked me some questions. We talked about my relationship with my dad and I opened my heart to him, sharing that I loved my dad and knew he loved me, but still felt like I couldn't get his approval no matter how hard I tried. Pastor James led me through some inner healing prayer, and it was powerful to forgive and release my dad so I could just love him as he was. I realized he had overcome so much, especially since he had been raised by a father who struggled with alcoholism. I still had a lot of personal issues to work through, but from then on, I took my faith seriously and felt a call on my life to help others.

I really wanted to change the world! At seventeen, I thought maybe I would be a police officer...it was the 80s and Charlie's Angels was popular on TV, and I had Farrah Fawcett hair after all! I realized quite early that I wasn't really cut out for the realities of law enforcement, so I decided that maybe I could be a counselor and help teenage girls. I knew how hard the teen years were for me and I wanted to help other girls through them. After high school, I went to a small Bible college, Lutheran Bible Institute in Southern California, where I followed two of my good girlfriends who loved it there. Learning the Bible and spending time at the beach sounded like a dream come true!

One of the first boys I met at LBI and had a crush on was Joel Midthun. I was a very loud and vibrant seventeen-year old, just turning eighteen when he met me. And he was a quiet, blonde haired, blue-eyed boy from Minnesota, who was also a missionary kid. Joel grew up in Madagascar where his family were missionaries until he was twelve. Joel didn't think I was his type but we became very close friends. I loved Bible college and my new friends, and I continued to grow in my faith. I also got very involved in the music program, playing the piano and singing. I loved all the opportunities to travel around with my friends doing music ministry and sharing my faith.

There was another defining moment that happened during that first year in college, when my mom called to prepare me for a call I would be getting from my dad. She said he was going through a lot of self-reflection and he wanted to call me. The transformation in my dad was remarkable, but he still had a hard time expressing his love for me. Often, mom would relay messages between my dad and I, as we had a hard time communicating and connecting. I was a little nervous and wasn't sure what to expect, but when my dad did call me, his voice was soft and humble. He told me he needed to apologize to me for being a harsh father. He said he saw a lot of himself in me and feared I had been making some of the same mistakes he made. He wept as he asked me for forgiveness. I could hardly bear hearing my dad break like this, but of course I told him I forgave him.

Through tears, I told him I realized that he did his best to love me and that he overcame a lot. I knew he didn't have a very good example to follow since his own father struggled with alcoholism. It was a sweet and precious phone call. I saw my dad continue to transform his life, and he was a wonderful loving father. It was so sweet for me to experience a good relationship with my dad in my adult years. I had been given an incredible gift—to see how God can redeem someone's life and bring healing to a relationship. A few times my dad and I shared our testimonies together, which always impacted people deeply. Dad shared his story with a group of men twenty years ago at a men's retreat, and those men still remember it and tell me how much that meant to them, even to this day.

My second year at LBI, I had just turned nineteen and was wrestling through my past hurts and pains. I thought maybe I needed to try counseling and scheduled an appointment with a therapist. That was the same week that we had a guest Lutheran pastor and his team come to our school to do a week of ministry called "Signs and Wonders." I didn't really know what that meant, although the previous summer I learned a lot about spiritual battles and witnessed some powerful things. My LBI friend Kathi and I had been traveling with a summer music ministry team when she opened up to me that she had been exposed to witchcraft as a young girl. We began to realize the way the enemy had influenced her and started praying against it when she started experiencing spiritual attacks and heard tormenting voices. It was so severe that there were times that she was being choked, punched in the stomach, and she even had marks on her body.

My eyes were opened wide, then, to the spiritual realm and the battle of the enemy in oppressing God's children as I saw my friend suffer. I was determined for her to be free and she wanted to be free, too. When we visited with my family in Arizona, a pastor at their church was experienced in spiritual warfare and encouraged us to come to the healing service. It was very intense, and I saw the power of the enemy first hand as I was attacked as well. I got very sick the night before we went to the healing service, so sick that I couldn't even sit up; I brought a pillow so I could lie down in the pew.

After the service, we went in a back room to pray for Kathi privately. This pastor saw how sick I was—my throat was so swollen that you could visibly see the swelling in my neck. He said to me, "you're being oppressed," and rebuked the enemy and the sickness, and everyone in the room saw the swelling in my neck go down dramatically. I was instantly healed. Then he prayed for Kathi, and she was completely freed from this demonic torment. It has been awesome to see Kathi and her husband Mark (whom she met at LBI) serve the Lord full-time as missionaries for over thirty years in various places in Asia. Joel and I are godparents to their two wonderful sons. I love that the Lord set her captive heart free and they are now bringing the gospel of freedom to the nations!

I was very hungry for the things of the Spirit as we experienced the power of God first hand that summer. We were all intrigued about this special "Signs and Wonders" week with Lutheran Pastor Joe Johnson. While he was teaching on the signs and wonders we had studied about, something crazy happened. We experienced the power of God that we read about in the Bible. Some of my friends were physically healed and others spoke in tongues, including Joel. We were blown away! We were learning new, intimate and powerful worship songs of healing that were coming out of the nearby Vineyard Church led by Pastor John Wimber (who had been mentoring Pastor Joe). Our small student body was being set on fire as we saw firsthand the power of God and how real He is! The last night of the meetings happened to be when I had scheduled my first counseling appointment the week before. I knew I needed help to heal emotionally, but I didn't want to miss out on the meeting with Pastor Joe, knowing that God was moving so powerfully.

I cancelled my counseling appointment to go to the final night, and at the very end of the evening, a woman on Pastor Joe's team stood up and said God gave her a word of knowledge (something we were also learning about). God told her that a young woman in this room had been raped and the Lord wanted to heal her. I started shaking and crying uncontrollably. I was wrestling with my thoughts, as I didn't realize cognitively that I had been raped but my spirit knew it was true. (Thirty years ago, date rape wasn't something we understood like we do today.) Pastor Joe came over to pray for me and my sweet friends all surrounded me and prayed for me too. I'll never forget as Pastor Joe wrapped his arms around me—I felt like it was Jesus himself holding me. He prayed that the Lord would release me from the soul ties from this experience and heal my heart. I had never experienced the incredible agape love of God like I did that night and couldn't believe that the Lord had singled me out to heal me. My heart felt light and free. It was pure joy. What a breakthrough that was!

A couple of weeks after that incredible emotional healing, we were all still on an emotional and spiritual high. One night, I was jogging in the park down the street from our school and it started getting dark. I decided I would go for one more lap even though I knew I should get back to my apartment before dark. Appearing from nowhere was a man standing in my path at a remote part of the park; I thought he was going to ask me something, so I didn't feel afraid at first. Suddenly, he grabbed my wrist and pulled out a knife and held it to my neck. I was frozen—his eyes looked demonic; they were literally yellow. But out of my mouth came the words, "Jesus loves you." I knew I was staring evil in the face and that this man was totally possessed. He forced me down on the ground, holding the knife to my neck, and started to sexually assault me. I remember looking up at the stars and thinking that this was it—he was going to kill me. But Psalm 23 came to my mind, the Scripture that my mom had taught me as a young girl, and out loud these words flowed out of my mouth as tears streamed down my face.

The Lord is my Shepherd, I shall not be in want.

He makes me lie down in green pastures;

He leads me beside the quiet waters.

He restores my soul;

He leads me in paths of righteousness for His name's sake.

Even though I walk through valley of the shadow of death,

I will fear no evil;

For Thou art with me;

Thy rod and thy staff they comfort me.

Thou preparest a table before me in the presence of my enemies;

Thou anointest my head with oil;

My cup overflows.

Surely goodness and mercy shall follow me all the days of my life.

And I will dwell in the house of the Lord forever.

When I finished praying Psalm 23, my attacker stood me up, walked a few feet with me—I could feel the point of the knife in my back—and he said, "RUN!"

I ran as fast as I could, sobbing all the way back to school, once again knowing that God had spared my life. I ran straight to Joel's apartment and collapsed and told the guys what happened. They called the police who came a few minutes later and I filed a report.

Although I was shaken, it was like my heart had been protected and I had peace. I can't really explain it, but I knew that because of the inner healing I had just experienced with Pastor Joe just days before, I wasn't emotionally destroyed by that sexual assault. I knew the enemy of my soul was trying to destroy me and I was determined that he wasn't going to win.

Another girlfriend of mine at the school was also assaulted just days apart from my assault. A man had snuck into her apartment on campus while she and her roommates were sleeping—she woke up to find him cutting her underwear off her. He was completely naked and she sat up and yelled at him and he ran. She jumped out of bed and chased him! In over thirty years, Lutheran Bible Institute in California had never had anything like this happen to any of the students. Again, we knew that God was doing a powerful work and the enemy was trying to steal what God had done in our lives. It brought us all closer, and we were even more resolved to fight this battle with the tools God was equipping us with.

The following week, the guys at our school were practicing soccer at the park where I was attacked. A bunch of us decided to go and watch them play. As we were walking back to campus, a house right next to the park had the garage door open. I looked and saw my attacker in the garage. He locked eyes with mine and I could tell he recognized me. I told my friends that this was the guy who attacked me and we hurried back to campus and called the police. This man was arrested that night, and soon afterwards, I was called to testify in court. It was an experience I wasn't prepared for at all. My dad came to support me, which was a great comfort. I had to identify the attacker in a photo line up and then get on the stand and testify to what happened to me. I was shocked and confused that his lawyer, the defense attorney, began to question what I was wearing and what I did to bring this on. I felt that he was trying to prove that it was my fault in some way. I just kept telling my story and I told the whole truth—what this man did to me was wrong.

The case was thrown out of court mostly because I couldn't identify the knife. Although I had a small cut on my neck, they found no DNA evidence on the knife that the police had recovered.

I had complete and unexplained peace, though. I trusted God in it all and that maybe being caught was a wake-up call for this man. Could God be giving him a second chance to change his life and never do this again? The police also said they would be watching him, so in my heart I surrendered the outcomes of this situation to God.

But something more important than I could have ever imagined happened. Something profound. I was empowered on that witness stand facing this perpetrator, who was only a few feet away from me.

I had found my voice again.

Song Story: Do Not Be Afraid

> *(NOTE: Stephanie wrote several songs throughout different seasons of our lives, and we will be sharing those with you at the end of each chapter. Some are available on iTunes and proceeds support Courage Worldwide.)*

A few of us musicians from the U.S. and Africa collaborated and wrote this song for Courage Worldwide's *Believe in Me* CD that I spearheaded in 2009. It's a song from Isaiah 61 to sing over our own hearts, as well as a powerful anthem we sang over the girls who are victims of sex trafficking. I loved it when our girls came to the Courage Concerts that benefited Courage House and I could see their lit-up faces as we sang, *"Do not be afraid! Never give up! You will display His splendor!"* Afterwards they expressed how amazing it was to hear songs written for them, and they were shocked that so many people came to the concerts because they cared about girls like them. And now, we see so many of these young girls in Africa and the U.S. who have been delivered from the pit of hell, conquering their fears, living a new life, displaying His splendor so beautifully!

"Do Not Be Afraid"

By Stephanie Midthun, Samu Githiomi,
Christine Smit, Cameron Stymeist, Ralph Stover

(Isaiah 61)

Do not be afraid, sons and daughters of our King
He binds up the brokenhearted, He will set you free
(repeat)

Usife moyo, never give up

Wanaume, wanawake, you should never give up
Do not be afraid, mambo yakikuendea murama
Do not be afraid, mambo yakikuendea murama

There's a love that is calling your name out
Don't you forget it now, don't you forget it now
For the life that was stolen for so long
All my people we all come together and say
I can't stand another day! God is calling and justice
Is coming around my friend, so you don't have to fear again

He binds up the brokenhearted—freedom for the captives
Release prisoners from darkness
He comforts those who mourn
Gives a crown of beauty instead of ashes
a garment of praise instead of a spirit of despair

You will display, You will display His splendor

Do not be afraid, do not do not fear disgrace
Promise you'll forget your shame
The Lord Almighty is His Name

You will display, You will display His splendor

P.S. Joel finally came to his senses and he realized I *was* his type! Eventually we married in 1988 and will be celebrating thirty years of marriage this year.

REFLECTION QUESTIONS

1. Is there an area in your life right now where you feel captive or stuck?

2. Read Isaiah 61. Do you have ashes in your life that you need to surrender and allow God to work? Reflect on areas where God has brought beauty out of the ashes of your life and give Him thanks!

3. What are the defining moments in your life? It's good to remember and journal about them, as they so often serve as clues to our destiny.

2.

Fight for Your Healing

OFTEN WHEN I SHARE MY STORY, THERE ARE SEVERAL PEOPLE, BOTH WOMEN and sometimes men, who come up to me to share their personal experience of rape, molestation, or sexual assault. For some, I am the first person they've told their story to. I am often asked how it is that I can share my story so openly. I tell them that this is what healing looks like and that bringing this secret to the light is what brought me freedom and peace.

It's heartbreaking to me that people don't feel safe enough to share their pain. They are so bound in their own shame that they think never talking about their abuse will somehow heal the pain. Here in Africa it's quite difficult because I'm told that there are so few people to trust that will keep something confidential. Someone told me that when they shared that they were raped with a pastor's wife, they found out that it had been told to the entire church! Counseling is not very accessible in Africa either, as there are very few trained counselors. It's why we have a vision to help bring training here for counseling and to eventually start a Trauma Training Center in Tanzania under Courage Worldwide.

Healing is such hard work and it takes a lot of courage to share something that's been so hidden in the darkness. Confronting those secrets and finding a safe person to process your pain with is key. I'm very pro therapy, but for me, through prayer and several safe people, especially my husband, I have found healing. It was a journey of many tears and hard work, and it was not instant.

Fight for your healing!

Do whatever it takes until you are free and at peace with God, yourself, and others. Sometimes a recovery program or support group can be helpful. It's important to choose a safe person or a safe church, where people can share their pain and know that it will not be told to others. I believe with all my heart that *victims can be victorious!* I have seen firsthand that healing is possible for one of the most traumatized populations in this world.

The Believe-in-Me Story

In 2003, God broke my heart for children living on the streets in Africa, and He called me to *do something* to help them. I responded by organizing benefit concerts for several years. In the summer of 2008, there was a strong sense from the Lord that there was something more for me to do in our own community of Sacramento, California. I had no idea what it was, but I knew somehow it was for children and I prayed all summer about it. At the time, we were in Southern California at our ARC (Alliance of Renewal Churches) Conference that our church was a part of, and I remember sobbing and lying on the floor during worship, praying to God and telling Him that I would do *whatever* He wanted. It felt heavy. And it felt big. I knew something was around the corner that I was called to do.

Just days later after coming home from that conference, I read the morning paper. On the front page of the Sacramento Bee there was a picture of a woman named Jenny Williamson. The article was about sex trafficking of children in our community. It went on to say that Sacramento was a hub for trafficking in the U.S. and that the FBI had recovered over two hundred children. I was shocked! I knew it was happening around the world and in far-away places, but I had no clue it was happening to U.S. children in our own country, let alone in my own community. The article stated that there were no places for the children to go once the FBI rescued them. Jenny's picture was front and center because she announced that she was going to build a home—a Courage House—for these children and call them family. Foster homes and group homes weren't working because of the level of trauma these children experienced, and most of these girls were chronic run-aways. Some had been placed in as many as thirty to forty homes. I tore out the article and it sat on my desk for a couple of days. I was disturbed at this revelation of trafficking in our community and I asked God if I was supposed to do something. Jenny's phone number was in the article and eventually I called her and left a message. Later that day she called me back and I found out that she received over two hundred calls! We decided to meet for coffee downtown that week. I had no idea how I would help, so I prayed that God would lead our conversation and show me what to do.

We met and I instantly liked her—she was actually louder than me (!) and had a charming southern accent. I was excited to hear that she had just gotten back from Tanzania, Africa, which had been a dream of hers to go since she was a little girl. We excitedly chatted about our love and passion for Africa and I felt a kindred spirit with Jenny. She told me about the non-profit that she had started called Courage to Be You, Inc. (now Courage Worldwide), and her passion to help people find their purpose since she had found hers at forty years of age after a mid-life crisis. She told me that she had recently heard a man by the name of Don Brewster of Agape International Missions speak and share about little girls being sold for sex in Cambodia—it was the first time she had heard the words "human trafficking." After hearing Don's heart-breaking stories, she found herself sobbing, writing the biggest check she could, and then feeling like she was supposed to help build a home for these girls. She couldn't quite wrap her head around the fact that she was supposed to move to Cambodia...how would her husband and her two teenaged sons go for that?

When she got home, she started researching human trafficking. Much to her shock, Sacramento kept coming up as a hub for trafficking of children. She found out that the kids were being rescued but there was no place for them to go—they needed a home. And then she knew that was it! That was her call—to help these kids find their purpose, to give them a home and call them family. Jenny unexpectedly found herself in the media when she went to meet the Brewster's to see how she should go about starting a home for victims of trafficking. A reporter happened to be there doing a story on their work in Cambodia, and when the reporter found out Jenny was going to start a home in Sacramento, Jenny found herself suddenly on the front page of the paper! The funny thing was that she hadn't even told her husband what she felt called to do! God had plans to start this ball rolling sooner than later.

I was so intrigued, and yet I still didn't know what I was to do. Jenny then told me that when the article was published, two adult women had called her and identified themselves as prostitutes. They both said something similar, *"It's too late for me, but please build this home for the young girls...they need someone to believe in them."* Jenny continued telling me that she had met a fourteen-year-old girl who was a victim of trafficking, who had said the exact same thing, *"I just need someone to believe in me."* Jenny said she was haunted by those words. I saw that she had been doodling the words *believe in me* on her paper. Jenny didn't know anything about my background other than that I was married to a pastor and loved Africa. Then she blurted out, *"I need a song, Stephanie. I need a song to tell their story."* I was taken aback—now I knew what I was to do. Jenny didn't realize that I was a songwriter and had done a benefit CD for street children in Africa. I told her all about it and then we both knew without a doubt that this was a divine appointment. We chatted some more and laughed a lot, and after several hours at that local coffee shop, we both got parking tickets! But it was worth it.

I went home with a mission to write the song, and three days later, it was done.

Song Story: Believe in Me

I wanted a younger girl to be the voice for this song, so I asked a powerhouse singer, Christine Smit, who was fifteen years old at the time, to sing this song and record it. I wanted this song to be the heart's cry of the girls who needed Courage House. Christine was perfect for it.

We debuted the song on January 11, 2009 at our church, and it was "National Human Trafficking Awareness Day." To our surprise, the media showed up and did a news story about Courage Worldwide and featured "Believe in Me." The reporter asked me how I could write a song like this and where it came from. I was able to share some of my story and my inspiration in writing the song with our local news station. That launched us into the community in a big way.

A few months after we recorded "Believe in Me," we completed the whole album, with "Believe in Me" as the title song. We had several talented local musicians participate in songwriting and recording, including my producer Ralph Stover. The musicians donated their time and their songs, even amazing Kenyan rap artist Samu participated, and he added a global feel to this album. It was an incredible project. We started doing concerts and people started believing in the dream and giving towards it. Funds were donated so that we could produce a music video for "Believe in Me," which was launched on social media.

The vision and dream of Jenny Williamson was massive—to open a home in Sacramento and Tanzania, and then to eventually open homes around the world where there were no homes for the girls to go.

An interesting side note is that no big businesses or mega-churches were interested in partnering with us in this fight against sex trafficking in the beginning. We had to prove ourselves first and their support came later. The pastors in Elk Grove who Joel was meeting with said yes to hosting the first benefit concert and $150,000 was raised for Courage Worldwide through their City Hope campaign. They believed in the dream!

I tried to get a national name artist to donate a song, thinking that would help launch this project and raise a lot of money. Except for Nashville artist, Phillip LaRue, who had a heart for this issue and who donated a song, for the most part it was an album of unknown artists with big hearts and who were incredibly talented. The music was powerful. The album featured songs of hope like "What if You Believe (you can change the world)," as well as songs that break your heart like, "Window," and "Believe in Me." We started to tell the stories of the children who were being trafficked and then God did something only He could do. Over the next year, during a terrible recession in California, we raised enough funds to buy a large property for 1.2 million dollars in Sacramento. A building was donated in Tanzania, and both Courage Houses opened August of 2011. Only God! We gave Him all the glory and knew this was of His heart.

"Believe in Me"

by Stephanie Midthun

She is lost and alone, waiting to be found
And find a place that she can call her home
Her innocence was stolen, her shattered heart is broken
Quietly suffering she cries…

Believe in me, believe in me
I'm longing for my captive heart…to be free

Daughter you are not alone—He died so you can live
He gives a place that you can call your home
The years the enemy stole, He'll restore and make you whole
He'll heal your pain and whisper to your soul

Believe in Me, believe in Me
I'll help you see what you cannot see
Believe in Me…I have come to set your captive heart free

Deliver her from darkness…rescue and redeem
Give courage and purpose, to live for you our King

Break the chains that bind her, let her spirit sing...
You are free and redeemed, Daughter of the King

Believe in me, believe in me
Help me see what I cannot see
Believe in me...I'm longing, for my captive heart to be free.

Believe in Me, believe in Me

Copyright © 2009 C2BU-Courage Worldwide/ASCAP

From Victim, to Survivor, to Overcomer!

While the team worked on the license for minors before the Courage Houses opened, we met three young women who were eighteen, nineteen, and twenty-three, and their stories were all beyond horrific. Each of them had been sold or exploited by their parents as young as six or seven years old. Nineteen-year-old "Kayla" was such a severe cutter that she had terrible scars all over her body from cutting and burning herself as a way to cope with her inner pain. She was also deaf, going blind, and had suffered from other tragic health issues. She wasn't expected to live past her twenties. It was as if her body turned against her from all the abuse. She walked through the doors of a church in Elk Grove and a caring young man befriended her in the young adult group. He called me to see if we could help her. We learned much about trauma from these courageous girls early on. They shared their stories with us and fought so hard for their healing. It was exhausting for them and for those of us trying to help. In the beginning, we couldn't find a counselor or a trauma therapist that knew how to handle their pain, but finally we did, and it changed *everything*.

Here is what we've learned about victims of sex trafficking. Our girls were almost all sexually abused as young children and then exploited or trafficked at young ages—some either by their own parents or other pimps (traffickers). Sometimes this was generational and their mothers were in the life, too. Some girls were victims of ritualistic abuse (witchcraft) both in Africa and California. Some were on the streets driven by poverty, and most were chronic runaways, either in and out of foster care or probation in the U.S.

In Africa, some were "house girls," tricked into thinking they were getting a "job" to support themselves or their families, but most often they were abused and sexually exploited. Recently, the Ministry of Home Affairs Office told us about a ring of five hundred young Tanzanian girls they had recovered from being trafficked to India as house girls. It's a massive problem that is growing daily. Globally, sex trafficking is a multi-billion-dollar industry with hundreds of thousands of children being sold for commercial sex. It's the fastest growing crime, second only to drug trafficking and tied with illegal arms. We are told that drug traffickers are literally changing crimes as it's more lucrative to sell human beings. (To find the most recent data, check out the Trafficking in Persons (TIP) Report the U.S. State Department puts out each year.)

Most of the girls have experienced hundreds or even thousands of rapes by the time they come to Courage House. Yes, you read this right—thousands. Often, they are sold ten to fifteen times a night. Calling it "sex" doesn't begin to describe what they experience. It is child-rape, sodomy, and torture—sometimes even with objects. One of our young girls in Tanzania was sold and sodomized by men at ten years old—apparently men justify it as being okay when it's sodomy where girls are this young. She has needed a lot of medical treatment to repair the damage that was done to her. It is heartbreaking and sickening.

We hope one day the label of "child prostitution" will be eradicated. These children are being prostituted and it isn't a choice any of them would make. Internationally by law, they are *victims* of sex trafficking if they are under eighteen years old.

"Survival sex" is a form of trafficking, too. Poverty drives a girl to the streets, or as we've found out, some parents or relatives tell our girls to go sell themselves to help the family pay for school fees or pay for food. This is also not a "choice." Desperation to survive does not make an eleven, twelve, or thirteen-year-old girl *choose* to sell her young body—she feels she has no choice. We recently brought a fifteen and a sixteen-year-old into our home in Tanzania. Both girls tried their best to stay in school but were so poor they would go to the streets to pay their school fees. The father had eleven children and he was trying to raise them on his own, renting a room in a mud house. Two of his wives had died and his third wife ran away. These girls are so smart, and in a very short time, they are thriving in our school. We are also grateful we can bring in girls with children—we have two girls with toddlers and two girls who are pregnant. Now the generational cycle can be broken in their lives and generations to follow!

What about the women—the adults; those who seemingly choose to be prostitutes? Many times, you will find that exploitation started at a young age, too, and they saw no way out. Or, there's a trafficker involved who receives most of the money and she is threatened if she tries to leave. Or, maybe she's trying to survive or feed her children or pay for their school fees, too.

Personally, I know what it took to overcome only two instances of sexual assault/rape and our girls must overcome hundreds or thousands of rapes. Most often, they didn't have a good family or their physical needs taken care of like I did. They all suffer from PTSD (Post-traumatic-stress-disorder), and complex trauma symptoms (i.e., flashbacks, nightmares, and something that we learned about called Disassociation Identity Disorder or DID).

Dr. Benjamin Keyes, from Regent University, taught us a lot about Dissociative Identity Disorder and how it is quite common in people who have suffered so much trauma. It's formerly referred to as Multiple Personality Disorder, a condition where a person's identity is fragmented into two or more distinct personality states. People with this rare condition are often victims of severe abuse, especially early childhood sexual abuse and trauma. It can look like "possession," and although the demonic realm can be influencing our girls, one of the keys we have seen in their freedom is finding the right therapist who understands DID. With that and prayer, we see incredible growth in our girls. It takes courage for them to face their pain and trauma, and when they do, we see a lot of breakthrough. The girls do fight for healing, and although they may have setbacks or want to give up at times, when they push through, they are very strong and almost fearless. They inspire us!

Sadly, many people who have been victims of some form of sexual abuse stay stuck in their pain and shame their whole lives. I believe that the enemy goes after children at a young age, especially in this area of sexual assault and molestation, because he can ruin and "take captive" someone for life.

At the beginning of bringing awareness to the community about the issues of trafficking and the trauma of the girls, we had many people tell us there was no way these girls will be whole again. Even in the church! Some said it was impossible for them to overcome the level of trauma they have experienced— they were just too broken. But we knew that with God, all things are possible and that is why we believed Him for the impossible. And we believed in our girls as they came one-by-one to Courage House. The good news about PTSD is that with good therapy, a healthy lifestyle, and a good community, it can be healed, but it takes time. There is no quick fix.

We have seen so much growth in our girls both in Africa and in the U.S. When girls are at Courage House for more than one year, 78% of them do not go back to the life of trafficking. But if they are at Courage House for less than a year, it is also true that 78% go back to life on the streets. That is an incredible statistic given that there is so much recidivism with trafficking victims. We are excited to see the results with our Courage House girls when they stay and embrace all that is offered.

To date, Courage House has been home to nearly one hundred girls in California and Tanzania. Joel and I worked with many of them—counseling them, baptizing, and praying for them, and some have called us "aunt" or "uncle." Here in Africa we are "Mama" and "Baba." Although there are struggles and set backs at times with some of the girls, we see many who are thriving. Healing *is* possible! Victims can be victorious! Freedom is our inheritance and Jesus does set the captive free, literally! There is nothing better than joining him in that work and seeing the chains fall off our girls. It's also important to meet their physical needs—providing a home, family, and good education. We want to help them to know their purpose and reach their dreams, and some are already living them. Some of our girls are moms now, and we are seeing them be good moms to their children. One is in the military, several are in college or vocational school, and many are working jobs and supporting themselves.

Our girls in Africa are telling us that they want to be doctors, lawyers, a social worker, teachers, pilots, a judge, nurses, a counselor, a journalist, and police officers. They have a purpose, a destiny, and an amazing future, and we can't wait to see it all unfold! Today, our first two Form 4 (high school) graduates in Tanzania just went to a three-month life-skills training program and will start further education this summer. Many of our previous girls are in their careers or are married with children. We feel like proud parents launching our kids and seeing their dreams unfold. At their high school graduation recently, the Lutheran Archbishop of Tanzania told these graduates, "Not only will you be a lawyer and a social worker, you will be the top ones in Tanzania!" The girls wept as he spoke life over them. Then he surprised them and honored them with a special goat that is usually reserved for weddings and special celebrations. We were all so moved, especially the girls. Giving honor to them when they've been so dishonored is truly healing to their souls.

As you can see, healing is possible but only when we fight for it. We cannot be passive and think it will just happen. We must be active and face the pain by processing it, praying through it, and journaling it. Finding a good pastor or a professional trauma counselor is critical. As much as I would like it to be so, healing from trauma does not happen with a single prayer. It can be a huge step forward, like it was with me, but that is just the beginning. I'll list some good resources at the end of the book.

I do have to say that many people want to work with our girls who are victims of trafficking because they have their own story. Often, like me, they've been through some trauma and they are drawn to help. But, we have found that many times people who come to volunteer or even come on as staff, haven't done their own hard work of healing. This can be true even with therapists and pastors. Some people are trying to heal themselves by helping others, and it can be both damaging to the one trying to help, as well as to the one being helped. If they have some unresolved pain, then working with our girls tends to manifest in unhealthy ways. Some people have even processed their pain with our girls, as if they are their peers, and this is not healthy or helpful, either.

Sacramento Law Enforcement Chaplain, Mindi Russell, did a great class at the Courage Worldwide Certified Volunteer Training. She told the attendees the difference between a "scar or a scab." A scar is a wound that has been healed but you remember it—a scab, on the other hand, can easily be picked off and bleed all over the place and it isn't fully healed yet. You see, if you have a scab when you are working with trauma victims, that scab will be opened up and it won't be pretty.

Be self-aware. Be honest with yourself in where you are. Ask others close to you if they see areas in your life where you need healing; then be open to listen. Those who go through healing may become incredible ministers to the hurting and the broken.

Fighting to be free may be the hardest thing you will ever do, but it will pay off in the end. Do not settle! Not only will you be better for it, but your relationships will be, too. God can use you in mighty ways to join Him in setting captives free when you are living in freedom yourself.

SONG STORY: I WILL BETROTH

My youngest sister, Christy, wrote this beautiful song inspired from the book of Hosea. We recorded it on the *More of You* CD, then did a remix and recorded it for the *"Believe in Me"* CD.

Hosea was the prophet in the Old Testament that the Lord told to marry a prostitute named Gomer, and although she ran from him time and time again, he was to love her and pursue her each time she was unfaithful to him. The Lord revealed to Hosea that His love for Israel and His people was like Hosea's love for Gomer—that He never gives up on pursuing His beloved ones even when we run away from Him. During the writing of this song, Christy was particularly drawn to the verses in chapter 2:19–20, in which God promised to betroth His people in righteousness, justice, love, and faithfulness.

"Betroth" means a pledge to marry, and no matter how unfaithful we are to Him, He continues to pursue us as His Bride. One of my favorite books by Francine Rivers, *Redeeming Love*, paints a wonderful picture of Hosea and his love for Gomer. We often find ourselves reminded of this beautiful truth as we love our girls at Courage House. Some will turn and run from love when they have only ever experienced broken promises and pain. But we are called to keep pursuing and keep reaching out in love. When the girls begin to receive the love that God has for them and realize He will never leave them or break His promises, we begin to see lasting transformation in their lives.

"I Will Betroth"

by Christy Eskes

Come as you are broken Child
I love you just the way you are
I will clothe you with My love
Come find compassion in my arms

Come run to My arms and I will hold you
Run to My arms and I will wipe your tears away

I will betroth you to Me, forever
Oh child, you're close to My heart
I will embrace you and love you forever
Child find your rest in My arms

Come as you are wounded child
I know your pain and see your scars
And I will heal you with My love
Come find redemption in My arms

You are sufficient in Me, My love will set you free
You will find all you need, if you will run to Me

REFLECTION QUESTIONS

1. Has trauma affected you (or someone close to you)? How is this affecting your current life?

2. Is there any area of your life where you see the need to fight for healing? Is there any way that you have given up on the fight or become passive? Ask God to renew your courage.

3. Are there any areas of your life that are more like scabs (partially healed) than scars (completely healed)? Ask God to show you how to find more healing.

3.

Warfare and Wholeness

"Be strong and courageous. Do not be terrified; do not be discouraged, for the Lord your God will be with you wherever you go." (Joshua 1:9)

THIS WAS A SPECIAL VERSE FOR OUR FAMILY, AS WE HAD MEMORIZED IT when I was pregnant with our youngest son and taught this verse to our two older sons. Our middle son, Matthew, was not even three years old yet. He had a little lisp and when he quoted this verse he said, *"YETH! Be bold and THTWONG and remember, the Lord is with you wherever you go!"* We found out that we were having a third boy and we decided to name him Joshua. One night, Matthew said, "I know what Joshua's middle name should be!" We said, "What?" He said, "1:9!"

A couple of years after Joshua was born, and just as we were launching our church plant Living Water Church, a man named Marv Quam called us. Marv was an older gentleman who also had an incredible prophetic gift and a huge heart for God and others. He was an unlikely prophet as he was a chain smoker with a raspy voice. Marv had been attending St. Peter's Lutheran Church, a traditional church where Joel was associate pastor for three years, when he started hearing a voice speak to him. He thought he might be going crazy. After doing some research, he finally realized he wasn't crazy and it really was God speaking to him, giving him special words of knowledge and messages for other people. It was uncanny how accurate Marv's words were. Marv was on the church planting committee with Joel at St. Peter's and when they were struggling to find a pastor to lead the new church, Marv said to Joel in his raspy voice, *"Joel, whenever I pray about the new church, I see your face.*

You are to lead it!" Joel, not being ready, told Marv to keep on praying until he saw another face! It didn't take much time for the Lord to confirm to Joel that it was indeed God calling him to lead Living Water Church.

When I (Stephanie) picked up the phone one day, Marv said, *"Stephanie, the Lord has a word for you and Joel for starting this church."* Marv said to read Joshua chapter 1 and focus on verse 9. Of course, I already knew these verses because we had recently memorized them with our boys, but I politely thanked Marv and didn't think much about it. When Joel came home that night from attending a party for the confirmation students, I told him that Marv called and told him about those verses. Joel was holding in his hands a gift from the confirmation students and then he showed it to me. It was a framed picture with Joshua 1:9, "Yes, be bold and strong and remember the Lord your God is with you wherever you go."

Well now, I was convinced that we would really need this verse! And we sure did! And we still do!

In chapter 1 of Joshua, it says *"be strong and courageous"* three times, and then one time it says *"be strong and very courageous."*

Over the years, the Lord reminded us through all the battles and the ups and downs of ministry and our personal lives, to not give up or quit and to let Him give us the courage and the boldness we needed to persevere.

The role of the enemy is to discourage us, in other words, to "DIS" our courage. He wants us to be fearful, weak, and to give up. And in the season of getting involved in the fight against sex trafficking, we were reminded of this often and asked for God to strengthen us, equip us, and keep us strong in the battle.

One by one, as the girls came home to Courage House in California, they started to open their hearts to us and trusted us with their stories. We were horrified at the level of evil they faced, especially the ritualistic abuse as young girls. Some had even been dedicated to Satan. Battling demonic forces became a regular part of ministry to the girls and it was exhausting. As we mentioned, we learned much about their trauma through Dr. Benjamin Keyes who came to Courage House at a time when we, as staff, and Joel, as their pastor, were being depleted of strength. He then educated us more specifically on the trauma and taught that everything we were seeing was not demonic. But, we do know the enemy was trying to wear us out and make us quit.

Let me tell you about two experiences that convinced me spiritual forces at work are very real. When we moved to Africa the summer of 2017, we learned that one of our girls at Courage House had been practicing witchcraft even though she said she had renounced it and decided to follow Jesus. We found that our staff was exhausted from some of the spiritual battles going on at the house—the executive team and the girls' pastor had been going to the house almost every night to settle things down. The girls were all having bad dreams and some of the girls were seeing demons. One girl, "Cara," told us that the girl practicing witchcraft had put a needle in her arm while she was sleeping. We learned it is common in witchcraft to insert objects into people "in the spirit," but I have to say we were a little skeptical. We were told that when people are delivered from witchcraft in Africa, it is common for them to literally vomit razor blades and other objects.

We asked Cara if this "needle" was put into her arm while she was awake or if it was in a dream; she said it was in a dream. Soon after, the girl accused of witchcraft wanted to leave Courage House, denying doing anything to Cara. We found a vocational school for her to go to, and peace and calm returned to the house after she left. We prayed for Cara many times for the next few months and she said she still felt the needle in her arm; sometimes the staff could see it and feel it too. Our doctor at Courage House ordered an X-ray and the technicians were shocked when they saw a 3-inch needle in her arm. The doctors advised surgery; we thought we were left with no choice. We also thought it would be a minor surgery with a small incision.

They operated on Cara's arm and could not find the needle; they even kept cutting to find it, but no luck! Instead of a small incision, it ended up being a 4-inch incision across her arm. They even sent her for X-rays while the wound was still open and the needle still showed up! They cut all the way to the bone but still could not find it. The doctor stitched Cara up and she came back to Courage House understandably discouraged and upset. We kept praying, but she could still feel the needle.

Two weeks after surgery, we prayed and took her for a third X-ray and it was still there! The doctor then referred her to a specialist at another hospital. The new doctor did a fourth X-ray and, yes, the needle was still there. The doctors were stumped and were trying to decide what to do. This specialist was a strong Christian and said, "We need to pray and seek God on what to do next." A few days later, Cara had a dream that a girl in a school uniform was behind her and said, "I'm finished with you," and pushed her; when she did, the needle came out of her arm. When Cara woke up, would you believe that the needle was sitting on the floor? She was so happy and excited to be free, and we were so grateful that God delivered her!

A few years ago, I (Stephanie) went on a business trip to Nashville for some key meetings regarding partnerships with Courage Worldwide. I was alone in my hotel room and had just fallen asleep when I saw a dark shadowy figure come from the bathroom and then was suddenly on top of me; he held me down and spit threatening words into my ear in a language I couldn't understand. I couldn't fully see his face but it looked like a middle-eastern man, although I knew it was a demonic being. I felt paralyzed and couldn't move or get any words out of my mouth, although I was praying silently, "In the Name of Jesus, I rebuke you and leave!" Suddenly, there were several bright lights flashing near the ceiling and around the room, and the being vanished. I sat straight up with my heart beating outside of my chest and called Joel to tell him what happened; I asked him to pray over me until I fell asleep again. I knew the enemy was trying to intimidate me, and although that was a crazy experience, I vowed not to give up or give in to fear. This experience helped me to know that the stories I was hearing from the girls about these demonic beings attacking them were real. I really get it!

We always warn people that if they sign up to be a part of fighting sex trafficking, be prepared for the powers of hell that will come against them. It came against us and our family, the staff, our volunteers, our girls, and even the organization. The enemy does not want to release the children trapped in this horrific darkness and will do anything to make us quit or to convince the girls to go back to their old life.

Rats and Garbage

One model that we had used for years I (Joel) had learned from Dr. Chuck Kraft's "Power Encounter" class at Fuller Seminary in the early 1990s. Most of the learning came, however, during the two-hour workshops that we students attended before class. There we saw that demonic activity existed even in seminary students. Dr. Kraft taught that demons were like rats and they were attached to the garbage in our life. Unconfessed sin, trauma, or unforgiveness are examples of things that demons can feed on. We can chase away the rats all we want, but if we don't get rid of the garbage, more or even bigger rats will come to the unattended garbage.

Jesus alludes to this truth in Luke 11:24–26:

When an evil spirit comes out of a man, it goes through arid places seeking rest and does not find it. Then it says, 'I will return to the house I left.' When it arrives, it finds the house swept clean and put in order. Then it goes and takes seven other spirits more wicked than itself, and they go in and live there. And the final condition of that man is worse than the first.

When we deal with the garbage first, the rats are easier to get rid of, and there is usually no big battle to cast them out. We learned not to escalate battles with demons but to focus on trauma counseling and inner healing, and when the girls were healthy enough, many times the demons left on their own.

There are five main ways that demons can be attached to us or have permission to have influence in our lives. The acronym S.O.U.L.L. developed by Marcus Warner (Deeper Walk International)[1] is a helpful tool:

S = Sin

Any ongoing sin or habit that one is hiding or unwilling to change.

O = Occult

Any objects, practices, or groups having to do with witchcraft.

U = Unforgiveness

Holding onto anger, hatred, or grudges.

L = Lies

Untruths you believe about God, yourself, others, or the world around you.

L = Lineage

Generational curses, sins, or habits that were passed down to you from relatives or those in authority over you.

Confessing and renouncing these realities significantly weakens a demonic attachment on a person's life. When the attachment is weakened, casting out demons can be done much quicker and easier.

LETTING WORSHIP LEAD THE BATTLE

There are many times in the Bible where worship or music is used to fight spiritual battles. From Joshua's wall-collapsing, trumpeting priests (Josh. 6:20), to David's smooth-jazz harp calming evil spirits (1 Sam. 19:9), to Paul and Silas's hymn singing that busted them out of prison (Acts 16:25), worship and music is one of the great tools God has given us to fight physical battles on a higher (spiritual) level.

Another one of these examples comes in 2 Chronicles 20:20–22.

Early in the morning they left for the Desert of Tekoa. As they set out, Jehoshaphat stood and said, "Listen to me, Judah and people of Jerusalem!

Have faith in the LORD your God and you will be upheld; have faith in his prophets and you will be successful."

After consulting the people, Jehoshaphat appointed men to sing to the LORD and to praise him for the splendor of his holiness as they went out at the head of the army, saying:

"Give thanks to the LORD,

for his love endures forever."

As they began to sing and praise, the LORD set ambushes against the men of Ammon and Moab and Mount Seir who were invading Judah, and they were defeated.

God had told King Jehoshaphat that they wouldn't have to fight this battle and that they just needed to trust God and watch what He would do. In this instance, the people of God decided to start worshipping, and God did the rest.

As Stephanie launched concerts to benefit Courage House, the musicians and worship leaders were doing more than just singing inspirational music. They were leading the battle in this fight against sex trafficking. They were singing over the girls and over the battle and declaring victory and freedom from the darkness. They were inspiring those who attended to be the hands and feet of Jesus and to be the army in the battle to set the captives free! Worship was defeating and ambushing the enemy, and we saw incredible victories over the many battles as Courage House opened and girls came home.

Many times, worship was our weapon of choice to free those who were being held captive. Sometimes as we simply worshipped in church, a living room, or at a Courage worship night, God did something—He collapsed walls of trauma, calmed strongholds of fear, broke chains of unforgiveness, and defeated enemies of peace.

Creating a culture of worship also did something for the girls at Courage House—it taught them how to fight for their own freedom by going to God themselves. They had direct access to God, and oftentimes, they had deeper experiences of knowing God's presence and hearing God's voice than we did.

During the heaviest season of battle, our church hosted a spiritual warfare training with Mayaba S. Choongo, a pastor from Zambia that Jenny Williamson knew. Mayaba shared her very powerful testimony—that she had found complete freedom and healing after thirty years of deep bondage to witchcraft. When she was delivered, she experienced a literal snake crawling out of her leg. Mayaba got an education in counseling and has helped bring freedom to many people who have been in bondage to the powers of darkness in Africa and around the world. She does a very powerful and balanced teaching for those who want to help others in bondage like she was.

Her ministry now is based on her three-legged-stool analogy.

The way to wholeness is to balance the three legs of inner healing, Christian counseling, and deliverance. Her teaching encouraged us by confirming the approach of the needed balance between these three modalities, which is also excellent for our African brothers and sisters since therapy is very uncommon and there can either be an overemphasis on casting out demons or no emphasis on this at all, depending on their denomination and background. (www. mayabachoongo.org)

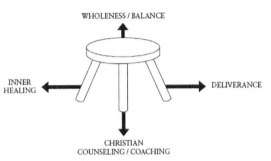

God brought us other great pastors to train us in inner healing and deliverance. One was Dr. Joe Johnson, the same pastor who prayed for me (Stephanie) thirty years prior and who has been a mentor and spiritual father to us all these years. "Papa Joe," as the girls like to call him, brought such a sweet and loving presence and encouragement to our girls and prayed for healing of their hearts and deliverance from the powers of darkness. He also did personal prayer appointments with many of the staff, as well as members of our church over the years whenever he visited. Many were healed and strengthened through his ministry.

Our friend and President of the ARC, Pastor Mike Bradley, has done a lot of ministry with our church and we especially loved the Emotional Health and Wholeness seminar he did for the CWW staff, which became our common language and core value. Staying emotionally healthy and providing resources for staff and our girls was extremely important to last in this often-difficult and draining work where there is so much burn out. (www. allianceofrenewalchurches.org)

Dr. Gil Stieglitz of Principles to Live By is a fantastic author and energetic teacher and has expertise in several areas that were extremely helpful. Gil was on the board of Courage Worldwide for many years and trained and equipped us and our volunteers in how to pray effectively, understand different models of deliverance, and other key issues like poverty, middle class and wealthy mentalities, and much more. His teachings were a game-changer and helped us to know how to more effectively help the girls. (www.ptlb.com)

What a blessing for us to have experts who cared about us, our church, our girls at Courage, as well as those who were working with them. These resources were invaluable to us, and God seemed to bring each person to us just at the time they were needed.

We have seen a shift in this balance approach for healing to the traumatized girls we work with. It takes courage for them to start a new life at Courage House and to face their pain. It also takes courage to work with these girls and face the battles that come to those of us who say yes to the call to help them.

We hope this is helpful to you personally in fighting your own battles or fighting for others. We all need to be strengthened and equipped to outwit and outlast the enemy and his strategies against us.

Be strong. Be courageous. Be very courageous! Speak this over your life and hear the Lord speaking to your soul when you feel weak and worn down. Deal with the "garbage" and remember the key of the three-legged stool—that balance requires inner healing, Christian counseling, and deliverance.

Worship the Lord with all that you are, and as you praise His Holy Name, watch the enemy flee and the walls come down!

SONG STORY: STRONG AND COURAGEOUS

We were struggling to write just the right song for the *Believe in Me* CD. We spent a whole day on another song and just couldn't get it right. That season was both an exciting time but also one with a big spiritual battle, as we launched into the community to bring awareness to the issues of sex trafficking. It was a battle to raise funds and to secure the properties to open the homes. We went home a little discouraged at the end of the day in the studio, and I told Samu that we need a battle-cry song. We got home and I turned to these verses in Joshua and Deuteronomy, and then Samu and I went to the piano and started writing this song and it just flowed. By the next day in the studio, it all came together! This song was powerful for our team… many times we sang this song over our souls, and we still do. We sang it at concerts and over the girls who were coming home to Courage House.

"Be strong and courageous! Choose life! Do not be discouraged! We don't know what to do, but our eyes are on You, Lord! He will fight the battle! Stand firm!"

"Strong and Courageous"

By Stephanie Midthun, Samu Githiomi, Christine Smit, and Ralph Stover

(JOSHUA 1:9, DEUTERONOMY 33)

Do not be discouraged, Do not be discouraged
He will never leave you, never forsake you

CHORUS:
I have set before you life and death
Choose life so that you, you may live
Be strong and courageous in Him
Be strong and courageous in Him

Do not be discouraged, Do not be discouraged,
He will never leave you, never forsake you Oh no Oh no
We have no power to face the enemy we do not know what to do
But our eyes are upon You Lord and that is why we sing

He will fight the battle, stand firm in the battle
Stand firm, have faith, be strong, He will deliver you

Yesu, Yesu, Yesu...Unaweeza (Jesus, Jesus, Jesus...You are able!)

REFLECTION QUESTIONS

1. Are you currently facing spiritual battles in your life or have you in the past? Reading Ephesians 6 and arming ourselves with the tools God gives us is a way to start. What current situation in your life is requiring you to be "strong and courageous"?

2. Do you think these battles are linked to any unhealed areas or "garbage" in your life? Ask God to show you as you work through the S.O.U.L.L. acronym.

3. Worshipping God through the battle is a powerful weapon and can bring great breakthroughs. It defeats and ambushes the enemy. Praise Him, worship Him, and lift up His name, and He will give you strength to overcome.

4.

Sacred Wounds

"I will return the vineyards to her and transform the Valley of Trouble into a gateway of hope. She will give herself to me there as she did long ago when she was young, when I freed her from her captivity in Egypt." (Hosea 2:15, NLT)

WE FIRST HEARD ABOUT "SACRED WOUNDS" FROM DR. JOE JOHNSON when he was speaking at our church one Sunday. He shared that *sacred wounds* are areas in our lives where we are wounded and, when healed, can be the very area God uses to help bring healing and freedom to others.

Understanding sacred wounds and how the Lord can use that healed pain for His purposes brought great fulfillment to me (Stephanie), as I was being called into bringing freedom to girls who had been sexually exploited and abused. It's like a kick in the teeth to the enemy, one where he has tried to destroy you in an area of your life and you turn the tables on him, destroying his work of death and destruction in others to bring them new life.

As a missionary kid (MK), who was born in Madagascar and moved back to the U.S. at twelve years old, I (Joel) found it very difficult to fit in to this culture. I was a "third culture kid" and many of us MKs struggle in life to adjust to a culture that is so unfamiliar to us. Many of my MK friends have struggled in their faith and, sadly, have even left the church. I have a heart for missionary kids as well as pastors. I understand what it's like being a pastor near burnout, who wanted to quit but got to the other side of it. My heart is to equip pastors and missionaries with tools to help them in their own emotional and spiritual health to help them avoid burnout.

We are going to share several powerful testimonies to inspire you with how the Lord uses these "sacred wounds" to bring hope and healing to others. We have seen how God has used the sacred wounds of many family members, friends, and church family in beautiful ways. They have given us permission to share their stories. We know that these testimonies prophesy hope; they are too good not to share!

DR. JOE JOHNSON

Pastor Joe lost his father at a tender age of seven years old. That feeling of abandonment and loss from his earthly father became an area where he felt God, our heavenly Father, had also abandoned him. Joe experienced deep healing from this pain, and has ministered to the "father wounds" in others for many years. He has such compassion and a gift in healing hearts. And many people love him, and they, like me when I (Stephanie) was nineteen years old, experienced deep healing and freedom. He also has suffered from depression and we will never forget when he shared his personal struggle with our church. He wanted to use his sacred wound of depression to minister to others who also suffered from depression.

First, he asked people who had overcome struggles with depression to come forward. There were several. Then he asked those who were currently struggling to come forward, and many did, even some that we didn't even know were depressed. Those who had overcome their struggle with depression prayed along with Pastor Joe for those who were in the midst of it. It was very powerful as he shared so openly, and how it brought the walls down so others felt safe enough to come forward for healing. Many lives were touched and healed that night. And a stigma of depression, that is so often in the church but never spoken of, was broken.

MIKE AND KAREN HERSCOWITZ

Mike and his wife Karen were part of our church plant from the beginning. Mike was a recovering alcoholic and a truck driver. He had battled his personal demons with alcohol and was passionate to serve God. When we felt called to bring a team from our church to Kenya, Mike and Karen felt called to go. Before that trip they had been having dreams of black children. They felt that they would somehow be parents to some, not knowing that they would be called to go on this short-term mission trip to Africa to work with street boys, many of them struggling with addictions to alcohol and glue.

After our mission trip to Kenya, they felt strongly that they were called to go there full-time. They sold their house and moved there to become the directors of the home. They had a beautiful ministry and were very good with the kids. Mike's deliverance and freedom from the stronghold of alcohol was his sacred wound, and he was a great father and mentor to these young boys and young men. He and Karen adopted a son who was an orphan and brought him back to the States to be a part of their family. He became one of our youngest son's best friends.

STEVE AND DANNA BUERGER

When Steve and Danna started coming to our church, they seemed to have a perfect marriage. People often called them "Barbie and Ken." We had a guest speaker years ago, and he shared with our leaders about how he had to overcome a battle with pornography and sex addiction. Later that weekend, Steve and Danna asked to talk with Joel and I. They shared that Steve had been battling a pornography addiction since he was eleven years old. Their marriage seemed like a façade to them, and they were starting to live like roommates with no hope that they could be free of this stronghold that had come between them. We admired them so much for being so honest, and we watched them fight for healing in this area and overcome this battle. Steve has been free for many years and they now have a beautiful marriage that is a testimony to others. They've been strong leaders in our church, and God has used them many times to share their story to encourage and counsel others—both married couples and men who battle pornography. Their testimony brings hope to many that freedom from this addiction is possible!

RANDY AND BETH SEEVERS

In 1996, we met Randy and Beth while Beth was pregnant with their son, Rhett, the same time that Stephanie was pregnant with our son Joshua. When Rhett was four months old, they got devastating news that he had Cerebral Palsy. Rhett was blind, deaf, and would likely never walk or talk. As he grew, everything had to be done for him. His parents lovingly cared for him day and night, but sadly, Rhett passed away when he was seven years old. They were completely heartbroken. I (Stephanie) sang at his funeral, and I'll never forget when Rhett's oldest sister shared how he was her best friend and how she could tell him anything. She missed him so much. Some thought this family might be relieved when Rhett passed away, but they weren't. His death left a big hole in their hearts. Turning their pain into purpose, Randy and Beth started their non-profit, "Runnin' for Rhett" and they now inspire tens of thousands of kids and families by sharing Rhett's story. They get the kids (and their parents) "moving into life." They've organized fitness training and professional runs.

Their sacred wound has not only impacted many in the Sacramento region, but their sweet boy is never forgotten, nor is their deep and unconditional love for him. (www.runninforrhett.org)

JEY MBIRO

We met Jey in 2009 when our church helped plant a church in Sacramento. Jey and his friend, Samu, came to the U.S. from Kenya to work with the church, as well as to fulfill the dreams they had for their lives. They were in a well-known gospel group in Kenya called *Zaidi Ya Mziki*, which means *More than Music*. Jey was a DJ with the group and both lived with our family for a season. Jey shared his story with us—he grew up in the slums of Kenya and was extremely poor. He got in with the wrong crowd and started stealing to survive, eventually going to jail as a young teenager. Soon after he was released from jail, God provided for his needs through Compassion International. Jey told us that the first time he ever heard the words "I love you" was from his U.S. sponsor. He was also encouraged that an education and a relationship with God were the keys to his future success. He said the letters from his sponsor meant the world to him and he had saved each one. It made us think about the boy we had sponsored through Compassion over the last few years and felt a little guilty since we weren't always consistent in writing him.

One day, Jey told me he had a dream to open an orphanage in Kenya and give back to the children since so much had been given to him. I had an idea, and I said, "Jey, let's call Compassion and see if you can help them. Maybe you could speak or do something to share your testimony since it is powerful to meet a Compassion kid who is now grown and is a success." He thought it sounded like a good idea, so I made the call and talked to someone at Compassion about Jey. Amazingly, they were just launching a program for this very thing. Soon they flew Jey to Colorado Springs, trained him in public speaking, and now for the past several years, Jey has traveled for Compassion International full time, speaking at churches and large Christian concerts and festivals. Many children are sponsored as a result of his personal story! We are so proud of Jey and love seeing him give back—he is also a wonderful husband and a new father. A documentary about his life is now being made in the film called *Mathare*. It will inspire many people!

ROB AND CARA LANE

Rob is our former associate pastor and now lead pastor of Living Water Church. He grew up not far from Sacramento, CA. When he was twelve years old, his parents had been having serious marriage problems. They sat him down and told him they were getting a divorce and he had to choose whether to live with his mom or dad. Rob's answer was nothing short of spirit-led: "A twelve-year-old should not have to make that decision." The next morning his un-churched family was awakened by Rob's dad, who said, "Everyone up, it's Sunday and we are going to church." Radical changes to every member of the family began that day and Rob's parents are still happily married over thirty years later. Today, Rob and his wife Cara minister to many couples with broken marriages through "The Marriage Lane," a ministry they run together that offers marriage counseling and couple seminars.

But their story continues! In their early twenties, Rob was a youth pastor for five years at a church in Redondo Beach, CA. This season of his life ended over conflict and confusion going on at that church, and they subsequently spent fourteen years out of ministry. They continued sharing their faith with others, and had a house church for a time. It was during this season, in 2010, that Rob first attended our church. He came in as a broken man—even that Sunday Rob came alone as Cara had taken the kids to see family after they argued.

Rob was left with a list of "to-dos" from Cara, one of which was to find a church they could attend when she returned. The other task was to hang up metal butterflies in the laundry room. As Rob was hanging the butterflies, he silently prayed with tears, "God, when is it my time to fly?"

Fast forward to March, 2017. We met with Rob and Cara (then our associate pastor for two years) to tell them of the call we felt to Tanzania. We explained that the elders desired to have Rob take over as lead pastor. After a few emotional and anxious moments, we decided to pray for them. Stephanie prayed, "Rob, God wants you to know that this is your time to fly." Rob broke down in sobs and tears when he realized that God had heard his prayer in the laundry room seven years before and answered it so completely and personally.

Louise Midthun Varberg

My (Joel) dad, Ernie, passed away from cancer when I was twenty-two years old. At the time, my mom, Louise, was just fifty-eight. My dad had just retired and they were looking forward to this season of life after serving many years on the mission field and as a nursing home administrator. It was gut-wrenching to find that the cancer he had in his eye twenty years earlier had returned and spread throughout his body. In six short months, he passed away at sixty-two years old. My mom (and all of us) grieved this loss and missed him deeply. After some months, Mom decided she would move forward in her life and she went back to school to earn her master's degree at Luther Theological Seminary in the area of "Death and Dying." Mom is a wonderful writer and the articles she wrote on the subject were shared with many who were suffering loss. She started leading a grief support group and her empathy for others helped bring many people through their loss.

Mom had been a widow for thirteen years when she met a man named Dale Varberg, who had suddenly lost his beloved wife of many years. Dale and my mom discovered they had much in common, and Dale was preparing a research paper on Mom's grandfather, who started the Lutheran Brethren Church that Dale had been a part of for many years. They met for coffee and later fell in love; they got married at sixty-nine and seventy years of age. This "sacred wound" my mom experienced helped many through their own grief and loss, and it ultimately led to a beautiful marriage. She and Dale have been married for almost twenty years.

Carol Martin

Stephanie's mom, Carol, was an RN who worked in ICU for more than thirty years. She was a caregiver at heart, but little did she know that she would need to care for my dad, her own husband, while they were just in their sixties. Dad had a devastating neurodegenerative disease that left him needing fulltime care before he was seventy years old. Mom tirelessly cared for him at home by herself with expert and loving care, but ultimately had to take him to a memory care home. She spent twelve hours a day, every day, with my dad to ensure his needs were met. She was also advocating for the best care for my dad, and she helped many other residents and their families walk through caring for their loved ones. People who visited my parents were very touched at her unconditional love for my dad, and it brought tears to many eyes. It was powerful to witness their vows "for better or worse, in sickness and in health" lived out so beautifully. Today, just a year after Stephanie's dad passed away, Carol is still reaching out and helping others who are going through the difficult journey of caring for a loved one who is very sick or dying.

Suzan Shoo

Suzan is our social worker at Courage House in Tanzania, Africa. When I (Stephanie) first met and interviewed her, she seemed quiet, gentle, and sweet; she was only twenty-six years old. I wasn't sure at first that she would be able to handle our girls, as they can be quite tough, and can even overpower our staff at times. I decided to give her a chance. Suzan was orphaned at fourteen years old and raised by an aunt and uncle; she knows the pain of loss and abandonment. Many of our girls are either orphaned or cannot be with their parents because of abuse and neglect; it's a deep pain they have to deal with. Suzan is great at helping them work through these issues and advocating for their needs—she has become an incredible social worker. In a short time, she has gained much respect from the head of Social Welfare in the Kilimanjaro region, as well as government leaders in the Ministry of Home Affairs Office. I tell her she is our "Esther" of Tanzania, and there is much favor on her life as she helps set captives free.

SONG STORY: SOMEONE IS WAITING

Both of my sisters, Carolyn and Christy, have beautiful and miraculous stories of adopting children. They both suffered through grief and loss with their miscarriages, and although my middle sister, Carolyn, was able to have three biological children, my younger sister, Christy, and her husband, Todd, decided after five years of infertility to start the adoption process. God brought four incredible children into our family in miraculous ways! Two girls were adopted from China by Carolyn and Brian, and Christy and Todd adopted a boy and a girl domestically. They could both write a book on their powerful stories! Carolyn is an international adoption social worker with Holt International and advocates for many children. Christy and Todd often encourage and pray for others going through the same issues they encountered. I love that my sisters openly share their stories with others to encourage people to adopt, and people have been inspired to do so because of them. These sacred wounds of my sisters have brought the most precious children, our three nieces and nephew, into our family—they are beauty out of ashes. It's a beautiful picture of how the Lord adopts us into His family.

In the waiting process for her first adopted daughter from China, Carolyn wrote a song that we sung many times at concerts as Carolyn shared her miraculous story of adopting Tessa. They had figured out that the Lord put it on their hearts to start the adoption process at just about the exact time of her conception. While the Lord was knitting Tessa together in her birth mother's womb, He was simultaneously knitting her into the hearts of Carolyn and Brian. His timing is perfect, always.

"Someone Is Waiting"

By Carolyn Cain

(ROMANS 9:23; EPHESIANS 1:5)

Somewhere someone is waiting
Though I can't see your face, I know your heart
Cause God has knit us together
Even though we're far apart
And until you can be here safe in my arms, I will trust
That somewhere someone is holding you close and keeping you warm.

My thoughts, my prayers are for you
Father love her, protect her, I know You do
And until that perfect timing when our hearts and eyes will meet
I will rest knowing You are there, I will trust
That somewhere, someone is holding her close and keeping her warm.

If time could stand still
Our love would bridge the ocean
But know that until then
That even the ocean can't keep me from you.

SONG STORY: FREEDOM SONG

In 2010, Liz saw the "Believe in Me" music video on Facebook, which tells the story of a girl being trafficked. She didn't know that anyone knew about girls like her and believed it was too late for her to get help. Liz was twenty-three years old and had been trafficked since she was only six by her own mother. Haunted by the song, Liz emailed Jenny Williamson, and with some encouragement, found enough strength and courage to leave her very dangerous trafficker at the time—a man she knew would kill her if he caught her trying to leave. She ran away in the middle of the night with no shoes, eventually finding her way to California. She moved into Courage House to begin healing.

When I first met Liz, she couldn't make eye contact with the person who was talking with her, and I noticed her face trembled when she spoke. She was sweet, smart, and had a witty sense of humor—and she was very deep. Liz told me her story and I couldn't believe that she could endure such evil and abuse. Liz thought she needed permission to speak as that was deeply engrained in her. We witnessed this courageous young woman on her healing journey and she fought so very hard for it. She was physically free, but for Liz and all the girls who come to Courage House, the hard part is then to be free mentally, spiritually, and emotionally from years of torment.

One day, Liz showed me her journals. I was honored that she would share them with me. She said that when she ran away, she started hearing God's voice. At that time, she had several journals she had filled with what God was speaking over her life. I was struck by the depth, beauty, and rawness of her writing. I asked Liz if I could write a song, using some of the words God spoke to her, and she said *yes*. This is our song, "Freedom Song."

"Freedom Song"

By Stephanie Midthun and Liz Williamson

I am the God who healeth thee, I am the one who sets you free
From the lies that have been spoken over you

I am the God who healeth thee, I am the one who sets you free
From the chains of death now broken off of you

Child believe, child receive
All I have I give to you
Child believe, child receive
My love, my Spirit and My truth

Just breathe, breathe in Me
Just breathe, you are free

Believe, Believe in Me
Believe, you will have victory

This is your freedom song
This is your freedom song
This is your freedom song

And now, I see Liz living out her freedom song...and her sacred wound is profound. It's been a beautiful thing to witness the many times I've heard Liz share her story publicly, and many people have been inspired to help fight trafficking as a result. Liz is also a mentor to other girls and is a big sister to many other young girls who have been trafficked. She gives them hope and can speak to their hearts and pain like none of us ever could.

NANGA'S INCREDIBLE STORY

Lastly, we met our Kenyan friend "Nanga" at our church, and she has one of the most heartbreaking and inspirational sacred-wound stories we've ever heard. We can hardly wrap our minds around what she's overcome and the incredible favor on her life as she advocates for the "girl child." This is a recent speech she gave before the UN, sharing her personal story, which received a standing ovation.

> "Child marriage and the subsequent domestic violence is a violation of human rights. Every day, girls around the world are forced to leave their families, marry against their will, endure sexual and physical abuse, and bear children while still in childhood themselves. This practice is driven by poverty, deeply embedded cultural traditions, and pervasive discrimination against girls. Yet in many parts of the world, this ancient practice still flourishes: estimates show that nearly five million girls are married under the age of fifteen every year, and some are as young as eight or nine years old. Child marriage and the subsequent domestic violence however, is not simply a human rights violation. It is also a threat to the prosperity and stability of the countries in which it is prevalent and undermines global development and foreign policy priorities. Child marriage perpetuates poverty over generations and is linked to poor health, curtailed education, violence, instability, and disregard for the rule of law. Its effects are harmful not only to girls, but also to families, communities, economies, and interests around the globe.
>
> I want to tell you a story about a little girl, let's call her Nanga. Her earliest memories were of seeing a car in her village for the first time when she was six. When she questioningly asked her mum, "Mummy, why is it that uncle Charly has a car and nobody else does?" her mother responded,

"Because he went to the white man's land and got a PhD."
So, at the age of six, Nanga decided that she would get a PhD
so she too could buy a car.

When Nanga was nine years old, she was married off to
a sixty-seven-year-old man in line with cultural norms of
wife inheritance. She was a child and little did she know the
horrors that awaited her. At eleven years old, after a traumatic
rape ordeal with this so-called husband, she got pregnant--a
child, carrying another child. Because the old man believed
that Nanga was the woman to finally bear him a son after
his six wives failed to deliver a boy, he subsequently gave her
favors—extra pieces of fish, so his potential son could grow
up strong and virile. Her co-wives were not amused by the
attention Nanga was getting, and one dark night, planned to
teach her a lesson she would not forget. Binding her swollen
feet and hands, they proceeded to beat her unconscious. When
she did not take water to her grandmother in the morning
as was her usual custom, her grandmother walked over to
Nanga's marital home to find out why. There, she found an
unconscious Nanga, bleeding and almost lifeless. With panic
in her voice, she screamed the village down and got people
to help her carry her grandchild to her homestead. There, she
nursed the weak Nanga, who unfortunately, or fortunately,
depending on who you asked, lost the pregnancy. Because his
wives had almost killed Nanga, the man who had married
Nanga was threatened into enrolling Nanga in school.

After her "O" level exams, she finished third in the country
and was placed in a government boarding school in the capital
city of Nairobi. This was an elite school and she soon found
herself out of her depth. For example, in the village, when
she was on her menses, she would go into the house and stay
there for the seven days a month it took to be presentable
to society again; here she could not. She therefore would
carefully pack chicken feathers, cowhide, and newspapers
that she could use during her menstrual periods when she was
in school. Her school mates soon found out and bullied her
mercilessly. However, her dream to get a PhD kept her going.
She was determined to overcome, after all, what was bullying
compared to the death that awaited her at home?

Finally, after a brutal four years, she finished high school, but her father would not educate her beyond high school. So back to the village she went and found that her earlier fears had become realities. Two of her sisters had succumbed to HIV AIDS due to the wife inheritance practice. However, her community called it *chira*, a curse, since they refused to believe that their cultural practices were slowly decimating their community. When another one of her sisters died, she being the oldest was told she had to marry him, in line with *tero buru*, the wife inheritance practice. However, Nanga, having gone to school in the big city, was aware of the dangers of HIV and refused to be married off. Nanga lived in a community where they would give her a small farm to provide food, and a communal water borehole; however, after an intense flogging in the market square failed to make her submit, they decided to starve her to submission. After three days of no food and water, she realized they were serious. Her options were limited—die of starvation or die of AIDS. She chose that which she had control over.

Under the cover of darkness, she fled, following the buses she knew would lead her back to the capital city. Her goal— to go back to school and get her PhD. She walked to the city for eight days going through many horrors along the way, but what kept her going was God's protection and grace. And every time she wanted to lie by the roadside and die, she would remember the dream of a PhD and keep walking. Finally, she got to the city. For the next two years, she lived on the streets living off whatever she could scavenge. There was an Asian lady who would come and give the street children food after praying at the mosque every Friday, and one day, Nanga asked her if she could work for her as a house-girl, and in return, would the lady pay for her school as wages? The lady agreed, however getting admittance to the university proved impossible since she never received her high school leaving certificate, her father having failed to complete paying her tuition. Shortly after, the lady's husband started a healthcare company. Nanga started as a messenger in the office, became the receptionist, then hungry for more, moved on to handle medical claims for Central, East, and West Africa. Her goal was to pay her *tuition so she could get her high school diploma and enroll in university to get her PhD.*

It was during one of these times that she met a man who she fell in love with and they had a daughter. Both Nanga and her husband played for the national team in different sports, and one year, her husband got an opportunity to do trials for a team in the United States. He left and took Nanga to his village to stay with his parents since she could not go back to her village where she was ostracized. Unfortunately, his community practiced female genital mutilation and soon, the whispers started becoming loud. Nanga was not a full woman because she had not been initiated as a woman and that was necessary if she was to be considered a legitimate wife. To give you an idea of what goes on with FGM, I'd encourage you to go online and see the reality of what some of these women go through.

Nanga refused to go through that because she had watched while her husband's sister bled to death after her FGM and her mother denied the opportunity even to mourn for her because the midwives who performed the cut said she was cursed. When Nanga refused to undergo the cut, she was told she was not considered a wife in the village and she had to leave; however, since the child belonged to the father, she was ordered to leave her child behind. That was unthinkable and so she did what she knew to do best. Nanga fled. Only this time, she fled to Uganda, a neighboring country where she felt relatively safer.

Life was hard because she now had herself and a one-year-old child to take care of. In Uganda, she thought herself safe, till one day she came back to the house where she was being housed and found her daughter had been kidnapped by the elders from the village. Somehow, they had tracked her to Uganda and waited till she was gone before they kidnapped her daughter and took her back to Kenya. Hysterical, Nanga went to the Uganda police who told her she was Kenyan and they could therefore not interfere. Her pleas to the Kenyan police elicited scorn and laughter. One policeman told her to stop behaving like a white woman and go do what she knew needed to be done. What they had not counted on was a determined mother's love.

With a machete in hand, Nanga cut through the forest where her daughter was being held and freed her. That same night, with her daughter whose arm had been broken, they made their way back to Uganda where they lived like fugitives, fearing for their lives. The elders in the village would not give up and came looking for them. One day, Nanga and her daughter were hidden under the bed when they came in and sat on the same bed under which the two were hiding. Nanga, with heart in chest was praying that her daughter would not as much as sneeze and alert the elders of their presence under the bed. That was just one of many hidings they had to endure. Things got so dangerous that the US embassy in Kampala got involved and that is how Nanga got asylum to the US.

That is my story and my life odyssey in Kenya, my mother country, where I was forced into exile for my resistance to the patriarchal and abusive policies of my rural village has inspired my life-long quest to learn, serve, and lead for global change in developing nations and communities ravaged by political oppression, gender inequity, and resource scarcity. When I landed in the United States five years ago, I barely spoke proper English, but I was determined to learn. I enrolled in community college in 2012, completed four AA degrees in one and a half years, was admitted to several schools, but I chose Columbia University because I wanted to work at the UN and Columbia was in New York where the UN Headquarters was. When I got to Columbia, I started applying for work at the UN, and the rejections came hard and fast. They all said the same thing. You have to have a Master's degree to work here, so I applied to the Master's Program at Columbia while still doing my BA and was accepted. So, for the last three years, I have been doing both my Master's and my BA, taking nineteen credits a semester, working with the UN and working full time on Wall Street because I am interested in the linkages between the private and public sectors. I graduated with my BA last May, and will graduate with my Master's this May, God willing.

My goal is to prepare for a bold return to Africa! I am

eager to leverage my education and dedicate my career to making transformative impacts on the world scene for women and girls—particularly in projects, organizations, and agencies which are rooted in fighting against domestic violence against women, environmentally sustainable development for women and the girl child, and expanding micro-credit for the elevation of women's status.

By UN estimates, one in three children born by 2050 will be African. More than half will be female. Will their fates be pre-determined by the oppressive conditions of 2016, or the liberated, empowered, and more promising conditions we can co-create for tomorrow if we commit ourselves today? That is the question. Leadership and planning for the answer, for the world that will inherit these children, starts now with me. My higher education is where I begin sowing seeds of hope, know-how, and empowerment throughout Africa. I give God all the glory; I would have died many times over had it not been by his grace. I do not know why he chose me, but he did and I choose to honor his name by helping others. I am not naive enough to believe that I can change the world, but if I can only change one life at a time, I will be accomplishing my life goal.

In closing, I'd like to give glory to God because I would have died were it not for his grace and today I have become the person I am by his grace. ARC is where my academic life began and is where I learned how to speak and write English and it holds a special place in my heart. So for anyone who is getting ready to either transfer or move into the job market, hold on and hold fast, make friends, network, and see yourself moving to higher places. I would like to thank my extended family that is the family God has blessed me with in the US. In the absence of my family, you have become my mothers, sisters, brothers, aunties, and uncles, and I thank you for honoring the work of women like me all over the world, because by honoring me, you have honored many.

Thank you."

"Nanga" has since completed her master's degree from Columbia University and one day wants to complete her PhD, but is focusing on her family now and working with Social Welfare in California, writing policy. She is on the U.S. Board of Directors of Courage Worldwide and is advocating to the United Nations on behalf of our Courage Worldwide girls. She came to Tanzania recently and inspired our girls, staff, and community leaders with her story. We can see she is a world-changer! In fact, the U. N. Delta also gave her the prestigious "Change Maker's Award."

All these people we have mentioned are beautifully "displaying His splendor" (Isa. 61), giving God the glory for all He has done. We are in awe when we see these people near and dear to our hearts use their sacred wounds to pay it forward to others. The beauty that comes out of the ashes of their lives is vibrant. There's nothing better than that.

REFLECTION QUESTIONS

1. Is there a "sacred wound" in your life? Are you able to see how and where this sacred wound can bring hope and healing to others? Have you experienced it yet?

2. Are there others who ministered or touched your life because of their "sacred wound"? Consider contacting them to thank them for how they helped you.

3. (If you have been unable to discover your sacred wound or you are unwilling to share it with others, we invite you to check out the workbook Uniquely You by Jenny Williamson for help with this, available on Amazon.com.)

5.

Worship and Mission

"If we lift our hands in praise and worship, but with those same
hands don't extend them to the poor and the needy, then we have
worshipped a singer, a song or a service. Worship makes a difference
in the lives of others." ~ Shaun Groves [2]

THIS QUOTE ROCKED ME (STEPHANIE). ACTUALLY, A LOT ROCKED ME WHEN I first went to Africa in 2003. I had been restless in ministry at the time, especially as a worship leader. I loved leading worship and had for many years but knew there was something more. I just wasn't sure what it was.

My two sisters and I had come together to write songs, record albums, and minister the healing presence of God through worship and music in 1999. We called ourselves Threefour:one from Psalm 34:1, which says "I will bless the Lord at all times, His praise shall continually be on my lips."

We were leading worship at a women's conference in Northern California in 2003. Afterwards, a lady named Darla Calhoun introduced herself and told me about her ministry in Kenya to street boys. She told me how they were treated as trash and no better than dogs in Kenya, and she had started a center for them called Agape Children's Home. She said these boys' lives had changed completely and they loved to worship. It was their tenth anniversary that summer, and she wanted us to come and do a celebration concert. My heart leapt, and I knew instantly I was called to go, even though for many years I had feared going to Africa. My husband was shocked when I came home later that day and told him I wanted to go to Africa. He hadn't been back to Africa since he was twelve years old and he wanted to go too. The timing wasn't right for my sisters, so we took a team from our church—the very first mission trip of Living Water Church. I knew I would be changed, and I knew God wanted to do something big in my life. Maybe this was it! God gave me a deep love for the people of Africa before I even went, and I couldn't wait to meet them.

I also prayed,

"Lord, break my heart for what breaks your heart. Move in me however You need to and change me."

When we arrived, it was shocking for us to see so many young boys living on the streets in Kenya, and yet I saw the hope that Agape was giving them when they came to their home and school. They went from being ragged, dirty, hungry, addicted to sniffing glue, and hopeless, to vibrant, strong, and healthy. Oh my, how they loved to sing and worship the Lord!

It brought tears to my eyes seeing them worship so beautifully with all of their hearts... some were orphans and many had been abused and/or victims of extreme poverty. The boys desperately wanted all visitors from the U.S. to know their names, which was no small feat as there were more than one hundred of them! I taught them the song *"He Knows my Name,"* and told them that I may forget their names but God wouldn't ever forget. He knows their names and everything about them. They would close their eyes, place their hands on their little hearts, and sing at the top of their lungs...

"He knows my name, He knows my every thought,

He sees each tear that falls and hears me when I call."

There was one little boy that especially got ahold of my heart. He was about seven to eight years old. He was living on the streets and lying sick under a tree, while other street boys were playing soccer. He was the age of my boys and all I could think of was how he needed a mother to take care of him. I gave him some of my water and quietly prayed for him as I rubbed his back. My heart felt like it would literally break. He needed help and Agape had no more room. We got up to leave and he got up with us, held my hand, and followed us as we were walking back to the center. I could hardly handle the thought of leaving him at the gate. I slowly let go of his hand and kept walking without looking back before we got back to the compound. I knew if I said anything or hugged him that I would break. When I got in my bed that night I sobbed. I felt so guilty for leaving him like that, and I was so overwhelmed by the needs, the thought of the millions of street children around the world. That little boy should have a place to sleep, to be cared for and helped—how can this become reality?

I cried out to God, "Do SOMETHING, Lord...how can You take care of all of our needs, yet these young children are calling out to You and they are desperate?" I heard God clearly say to me, *"Stephanie, I want YOU to do something. You can be their voice and My hands and My feet. There is something for YOU to do."*

I was also deeply struck by God's manifest presence being so strong as we sat with the street boys under the tree at the park. I thought of Jesus talking about the "least of these" in Matthew 25:

> "For I was hungry and you gave me something to eat, I was thirsty and you gave me something to drink. I was a stranger and you invited me in. I needed clothes and you clothed me. I was sick and you looked after me. I was in prison and you came to visit me. Whatever you did for one of the least of these brothers of mine, you did for Me."

You see, loving the most vulnerable and needy, giving them something to eat and drink. and providing for their physical needs was actually doing this to Jesus himself. This was why I felt his presence so strongly...and this was a revelation to me. This was worship. And this was what I had been missing.

These verses in Isaiah jumped out to me when I sat with the Lord about our time in Africa:

> "Is this the kind of fasting I have chosen: to loose the chains of injustice and untie the cords of the yoke, to set the oppressed free and break every yoke? Is it not to share your food with the hungry and to provide the poor wanderer with shelter - when you see the naked to clothe him and not turn away from your own flesh and blood? Then your light will break forth like the dawn, and your healing will quickly appear; then your righteousness will go before you, and the glory of the Lord will be your rear guard. Then you will call and the Lord will answer; you will cry for help and he will say; Here am I. If you do away with the yoke of oppression, with the pointing finger and malicious talk, and if you spend yourselves on behalf of the hungry and satisfy the needs of the oppressed, then your light will rise in the darkness, and your night will become like the noonday. The Lord will guide you always; he will satisfy your needs in a sun-scorched land and will strengthen your frame. You will be like a well-watered garden, like a spring whose waters never fail. Your people will rebuild the ancient ruins and will raise up the age-old foundations. You will be called Repairer

of Broken Walls; Restorer of Streets with Dwellings." (Isaiah 58:6–14)

I came home from Africa a complete mess. My sisters and I went right into recording a worship album and a Christmas album, which we had previously planned to do. I couldn't stop talking about Africa and wanted to make every song of ours about it. After many tears and lots of prayer and encouragement from my sisters, they suggested that I spearhead a separate benefit CD and they wanted to be a part of it. I knew this was what I was supposed to do. Our church caught the vision and supported us. They gave financially, and musicians from our church participated. I flew back to Kenya with my producer, Ralph Stover, and we recorded the kids singing "He Knows My Name" (the title song of the album) and other songs, some they had written, and we produced a music video called "The Least of These."

We did many benefit concerts to tell the story of these children. I wanted people to experience the heartbreak and to inspire them with hope that we can do something. Each of us has a part to play in this broken world. We raised funds so that many more children could be helped. We love the ministry of Agape Children's Ministry in Kisumu, Kenya, and they continue to thrive in their cutting-edge work with street children as their ministry has expanded. They've had unprecedented success reintegrating-to-date over 2,500 street boys and girls back into their home villages, where they thrive in school and with their relatives. They've expanded their services to girls and to other locations. We have been so very blessed to be a part of the movement of God for these most vulnerable ones in Kenya. (www.agapechildren.org)

This forever changed what I think of as worship. Like Sean Groves said, our worshipping God should be making a difference in the lives of others. It's not just a vertical relationship with Him, but it is horizontal, as well. It should be meeting the needs of His people, which touches the very heart of Jesus himself.

WE COULD HAVE MISSED THIS

I also think of a couple at our church, Matt and Traci Feaster, who we've known for more than twenty years; they were in our college group, Joel married them, and they've been friends, faithful leaders, and passionate worshippers. They already had three beautiful daughters when God broke their hearts for the orphaned children in Haiti after the big earthquake a few years ago that left many children orphaned. As they watched the news in horror, they knew they needed to do something. They researched how to adopt children in Haiti and found the doors were closed because of the trafficking issues that the government needed to sort out. I asked my sister about all of this, as she is an international adoption social worker. Carolyn told them that Haiti is closed but that Ethiopia was wide open for adoptions. After praying about it, Matt and Traci knew that adopting from Ethiopia was what God was calling them to do. They started the long adoption process and our church helped to raise funds; God provided miraculously every step of the way.

They adopted a beautiful son, Misgana, which means "thanksgiving or giving thanks." Even his name means worship! They called him "Ty" and we were so honored when they asked us to be his godparents. What an inspiration this couple has been to so many others, and we've seen several families at our church adopt since then, including Matt's sister. A few years after they adopted Ty, Matt was on a mission trip to Ethiopia. During that time, we became aware of a young woman who was in jail and pregnant. She wanted to get her life together when she was released from jail and needed help with her baby for a few weeks until her release. We asked Traci if she thought she and Matt could take this child for a short time. Traci's heart was compelled to do this and she contacted Matt just before he boarded a plane to come home. She asked him what he thought. He reluctantly said "yes," *if* it was temporary and they would help with the baby for no more than five weeks! Matt emphasized this several times. He was putting his foot down! Four kids were plenty, according to Matt. We were just relieved to find a good temporary home for this little one and eager to see the birth mom get her life in order, so she could be reunited with her precious little girl.

Matt and Traci's family all fell in love with little Lily, including Matt, who tried not to get too attached. When the time came to take her back to her birth mom, they were full of mixed emotions. They grew to deeply love this little girl, but they knew she needed her birth mom. Sadly, this young woman started to struggle and went back to her old dangerous life. It became clear that little Lily was not being taken care of. Matt and Traci were devastated and felt totally helpless. A couple of weeks had passed, and the situation got more difficult as they were learning that Lily's birth mom was making dangerous decisions and Lily was not safe. One night, Matt and Traci and their children were crying out to God, crying and praying that He would rescue Lily. Right after a powerful family prayer time, Child Protective Services became involved and it was a miraculous rescue of this sweet baby who was reunited with the Feaster's just a couple of weeks after they gave her back to her birth mom. It wasn't long after this and through some ups and downs and twists and turns that God made a way for Lily to be adopted by Matt and Traci, now her forever family. She has been given a new chance at life and is growing up loved, cared for, and knowing Jesus. We all still pray for Lily's mama, with hope and faith that one day she may be able to be in Lily's life again. Traci often posts pictures of this sweet, spunky, and spicy little girl with our new favorite hashtag, #wecouldhavemissedthis.

SONG STORY: JUSTICE GENERATION

I read the book called *Just Courage*[3] by Gary Haugen of International Justice Mission (IJM), who does fantastic work in fighting trafficking around the world. He said God is displeased with worship that doesn't include the ministry of justice. God is appalled when His church doesn't show up to stop the injustices.

> "Away with the noise of your songs! I will not listen to the music of your harps. But let justice roll on like a river, righteousness like a never-failing stream!" (Amos 5:23–24)

> "When you spread out your hands in prayer, I will hide my eyes from you; Even if you offer many prayers, I will not listen."

> "Stop doing wrong, learn to do what is right! Seek justice, encourage the oppressed, defend the cause of the fatherless, plead the cause of the widow." (Isaiah 1:14–17)

Gary used the words "justice generation" as the description of the generation that wants to get out of the pews and the walls of the church and make a difference in this world. It inspired me to write this worship song with my friend Cameron Stymeist, and singer/songwriter Aimee Bellanca sang on the vocal with him on our *Believe in Me* album for Courage House.

"Justice Generation"

By Stephanie Midthun and Cameron Stymeist

God of justice, God of love
God of mercy who rescues us
We lift our hearts to you and sing
We praise your name

God of kindness, God of peace
God of beauty, fall on me
God of every living thing
We praise your name
Let us be a justice generation
We will bring Your hope to every nation
We will be Your hands and be Your feet
God we sing

We will be Your hands we will be Your feet
We will love the lost and the least of these
We lift up our hearts and our hands to You we sing
God we sing

REFLECTION QUESTIONS

1. Read and reflect on Matthew 25 about the "least of these," along with Isaiah 58.

2. How has your worship of God moved you to minister to the least of these? Who is it that God may be leading you to reach out to?

3. What is the biggest fear or obstacle keeping you from total surrender to God's will?

6.

Winning Is Not Quitting

"I'm over it..."

Aﬁﬂﬂ over thirty years of working in some form of ministry, I (Joel) can't count how many times I have said and heard these phrases: *"Feeling done." "Did we hear God right?" "What are we doing?" "I'm over it..."* or, *"I wish I just had a normal job."*

Every young pastor thinks he or she is ready for the ministry—ready to fight the enemy, save the lost, stand for justice, and preach the word of God. Most have been trained in theology, ancient languages, how to preach, and do church administration. They are ready for the battle—or are they?

What they haven't been taught is how to handle the emotional highs and lows of ministry. And while they will share in the joy of someone's new baby, new marriage, or new faith, they will also share in the pain of their divorce, a new diagnosis, their son's drug problem, or somebody's death.

They also haven't been shown how to cope when a close friend or colleague betrays them, or what to do when a respected leader has turned against them. They aren't prepared for how their marriage will be tested and the pressures their children will feel. These are the things that can make you want to quit... the things you didn't expect, the things that blow your theology to pieces.

This Will Never Happen to Us

As a young pastor who was contemplating starting a new church in 1999, this was Stephanie's and my discussion one day as we dreamed and planned. Whenever we remembered difficult or painful experiences with leaders and organizations we had worked with, we were glad these things would never happen to us. And if we are honest, when it came to raising our sons, we also quietly thought that we would be better parents than some others. Why? *Because we were going to do it differently.* We would love better, pray more, stay humble, and learn from others' mistakes. We had it all figured out. Or so we thought.

Then It Happened to Us

Our church was seven years old when the bottom fell out. Within a period of one year, we were reeling from what seemed like a multitude of "plagues" surrounding us. After six great and inspirational annual congregational meetings, our seventh one was filled with questions, doubt, fear, and tension. After years of unified leadership and close friendships, two elders resigned and a group of members left our church. After years of good relationship with our denomination, we received pressure and criticism from them. After years of good health, we faced multiple illnesses: an aggressive staph infection within our family, where Stephanie and one of our sons had to be hospitalized, and Joel and another son had severe cases and were almost hospitalized. After successfully parenting three boys who were doing well, we suddenly found ourselves in a family crisis. One teenage son was being dismissed from a Christian high school because he was selling drugs, and another son was sick and struggling with such severe anxiety and depression that it was a battle for him to go to school each day.

Several members in our church were facing life threatening illnesses as well, and the more we prayed for them, the sicker they got. Two women died from cancer...one in her 40's with two young children and one in her 50's. One of our newest members, Ava, a 25-year-old new Christian that Stephanie was mentoring, got very sick with an aggressive form of Multiple Sclerosis (MS) and became paralyzed from the neck down in a matter of months.

In spite of our resolve, this *did* happen to *us!* We felt confused about why God would allow all of this at once, and why others, especially some of our closest friends, would treat us badly. We felt the searing pain of betrayal from those we cared about, the nagging doubt of our call to ministry, the fear of failure, and fear of the future. We felt like we were failing our kids and wondered, "Where had we gone wrong?" It was all just too much.

We Wanted to Quit

We asked ourselves many questions during this season, wondering if we had done something wrong—if the enemy was attacking, or maybe it was a combination of both. We also wanted to defend ourselves from the lies that were being spread. But the Lord told Stephanie clearly that during this season we were to let Him be our Defender and to stay on our knees in prayer.

God provided ministry to our hearts in unexpected ways. Our church had an annual women's retreat and we hosted Denise Siemens from Arise! Women's Ministry as our speaker. Denise, who was a friend of ours, shared transparently about the pain she and her pastor husband went through in ministry with betrayals and a very dark season they went through with their daughters. Her words and message brought such encouragement to all of us, and she was the first one we called for her wisdom, counsel, and prayers.

Stephanie also met a speaker at another women's retreat where she and her sisters were singing. This woman (a pastor's wife) had shared with the group about her and her husband's story of betrayal in their church and their son's tragic accident. Out of that season, their sacred wounds, they started a ministry for pastors and leaders. Stephanie approached her to see if we could come and stay with them at their ministry house, and this woman responded, "The Lord told me already that you and your husband are supposed to come to see us for a few days." This pastoral couple's small church owned a cozy little house near the church for the purpose of hosting pastors, missionaries, and ministers who are burned out, exhausted, or wounded.

They loved us and took us to dinner, listened to us, challenged us, prayed for us, anointed us, and gave us prophetic words. Most of all, they reminded us of who we were! God was still calling us. After two days, we left restored with a new confidence and sense of calling. We returned ready for a new season of ministry but with a new (and healthier) awareness of how little we could control the outcomes in life and in people. And as humbling as it was, this *could* and *did* happen to us. We weren't above or beyond it at all.

We eventually saw things change and God moved in some powerful ways. Ava, who had become a powerful prayer warrior for us and our church while she was in her own health crisis, was miraculously healed from MS! Years later, she is healthy and now a young mother. Our son, who had been dismissed from high school, became a passionate follower and worshipper of Jesus. Our other son has worked very hard to overcome his personal struggles as well. So, the battles turned into breakthroughs in many areas. This season kept us humble, made us more dependent upon God, and made us very protective of the unity of our church. Unity is a precious gift, but it can also be costly.

STAYING OUT OF THE TRIANGLE

As we got more involved in working with victims of human trafficking, initially Stephanie and I were some of the first responders when the girls struggled with breakdowns and emergencies. Whether it was driving to Courage House anytime night or day to pray for them, exploring seedier areas downtown searching for a girl who had run from the home, or taking various girls temporarily into our home, we were hooked. We could never say no—after all, how could we? We had time and resources, and they needed them, so we gave and gave and gave until we, along with most of the Courage staff, were tired and overwhelmed.

We also saw another pattern over time that we could not comprehend. Whether it was the girls, the volunteers, or the staff, many came into the organization loving the mission, loving the leadership, and were excited to be a part of the call to "fight trafficking." Girls were happy to be "home," and the dream was unfolding. There was incredible life change in the girls; the volunteers and staff were fulfilled to be a part of the team. But after a few years, we saw many of the girls turn against staff, or staff turn against the leadership, and it was confusing to watch or be a part of it. We had never seen such a love/hate dynamic to this extreme in ministry.

Thankfully, insight into this crazy cycle came one day from psychologist Dr. Vanessa Snyder, who worked closely with Courage Worldwide. She told the leadership team about the Trauma-Drama Triangle, based on the book *The Power of TED: The Empowerment Dynamic* by David Emerald. This is a normal dynamic that is seen when working with trauma victims.[4] "You're in the triangle," she said. "The what?" we asked. "The trauma-drama triangle." It seems that whenever someone has been through severe trauma over a long period of time, they learn to survive by categorizing everyone in their lives into one of three roles: rescuer, victim, and perpetrator (persecutor). This is based on their perspective, not reality—but it is their reality. Usually they see themselves as the victim and you as the rescuer, but that can and will shift over time. And whenever they change roles, you change roles, too (in their mind). Throw in the secondary trauma that happens to the people who work closely with the victims, and we found ourselves in a "perfect storm."

THE TRAUMA–DRAMA TRIANGLE

What is a victim? A victim's mindset is "poor me." Their focus is on their past hurts, failures, and disappointments. They feel hopeless, powerless, and full of shame. This leads to an inability to make decisions, take responsibility, or actively use problem-solving skills. It is hard for them to feel sustained pleasure or joy in life, and they tend to make excuses for inaction. To get what they need, they become manipulators and passive-aggressive. A victim's biggest

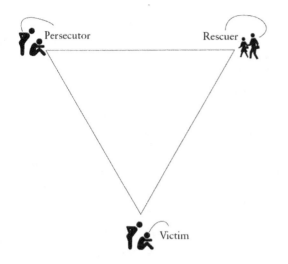

fear is getting hurt again, so why try? Trying leads to two things that a victim cannot stand: disappointment and accountability.

What is a rescuer? A rescuer's mindset is "let me help you." They are focused on the hurts of others. They feel guilty if they are not continually doing something constructive to help others. Oftentimes, they are unconsciously helping others in an attempt to heal or avoid their own unresolved issues. This often leads to enabling victims to remain dependent on them. It gives the unspoken message to the victim that they are powerless without the rescuer in their life. Instead of leading to freedom, this unhealthy cycle keeps the victim in bondage longer than necessary. The rescuer's biggest fear is loss of purpose: "If I'm not accomplishing anything or helping others, why am I here?" Keep in mind that a rescuer doesn't always have to be a person; addictions to alcohol, drugs, sexual addiction, and workaholism are all ways to numb us and rescue us from our negative emotions.

What is a persecutor? A persecutor's mindset is "it's all your fault." Their focus is on blaming others. They are critical, oppressive, angry, rigid, and superior. They survive by controlling and/or abusing others physically, emotionally, or spiritually. Their fear is loss of control. Oftentimes, they have been a victim themselves as a child and have unconsciously decided to become a persecutor rather than stay a victim as an adult.

What does this look like in real life? When you first begin helping someone, he or she usually is often a genuine victim and you are a compassionate person who wants to rescue them and help them have a better life. Most of us in ministry are rescuers but soon this can become distorted. As you begin to set healthy boundaries or accountability that is foreign to the victim, they begin to resist. To your surprise, they will begin to see and treat you as their persecutor instead of their rescuer. Now you have changed roles (without your knowing), but you are still in the triangle! Next, you may get impatient and inwardly angry that they are not gratefully receiving your help, but now you have really moved to be a persecutor; they are still the victim and you are still in the triangle! What can happen is that the person you are trying to help moves away from you to find a new and improved rescuer. We have seen some people move from person to person, church to church, non-profit to non-profit, and group home to group home looking for the person to tell them what they want to hear. They will find someone else to tell them that they are still a helpless victim and agree with how you were such a mean persecutor.

As new girls would come into the home, the older ones would naturally go into rescuer or persecutor role, while the new girls fulfilled the role of victims. One of our girls, "Brenda," was thriving during her first year at Courage House in California. Soon after her transition to college, she made some unhealthy choices and slowly started down the path of drugs, and even went back to the life for a bit. She very much needed good trauma therapy and had reached out for help at one point; but a family mentoring her at the time was convinced God would heal her if she prayed and worshipped enough. Brenda wanted my colleague and I to talk to them and we did, but they completely disagreed that Jesus alone wasn't enough to deliver and free her. Brenda desperately needed expert trauma therapy from someone who understood DID. Sadly, she went back to the life and then started recruiting other girls. She unknowingly took on the "persecutor" role in the triangle, which, like we said, is common for this population.

After that, she was nearly killed in a brutal rape that required surgery from the attack. It was heartbreaking to us to see this path she was on but we knew this could be a defining moment for her. At this point Courage was trying to help her by finding an aftercare home but she could only go if she was clean and sober. She was looking also for other rescuers and began to reach out to other non-profits in the area for resources; some of them were jumping in to help her. It was unhelpful in that it was like pitting parents against each other, with Courage as the bad parent because she was being held accountable for her choices. It feels good to be a "rescuer," and as a "victim" it feels good to be rescued. What Brenda needed was to rescue herself—to make healthy choices and get into a recovery program with expert trauma therapy. Today, she is fighting hard for her freedom with all she's got, and we are confident that she will continue to overcome! She has a heart to help others fight for their freedom and shares her story to inspire them to not give up.

This dynamic can also happen in other places than working with trauma victims. Our eyes were opened to see how prevalent the trauma-drama triangle can happen in the church or even in your own family, like it did with ours.

Our firstborn son was successful at whatever he did. He excelled at academics, sports, and music—and he was always the winner of the "Mr. Hussle" award on any sports team he played on. He is a hard worker and the guy that everyone likes and wants to hang around. At seventeen, however, he got sick with a very severe case of mononucleosis. In just a few months, this sickness that took us a year to diagnose, sapped his confidence, affected his ability to focus, and left him fighting severe depression and anxiety. Even his strong faith in God was challenged, as countless prayers for healing seemed unheard or unanswered.

Counseling and medication didn't seem to help, and after struggling to live on his own, we decided together to have him move back home with us—on *one* condition that he save money and attend college. After a few months of struggling in college and accumulating zero savings, I was starting to feel stressed and frustrated. You see, I (Joel) was trying to become his "rescuer" and it wasn't working. This made me feel like a failure as a man, a father, a husband, and a pastor.

In my mind, he was the "victim" and all I saw at that time was that he was not taking initiative for his life. When I came home and saw his car parked on the street by our house, I began to feel stress and anger. I was moving from "rescuer" to "persecutor" without him or I even knowing it. After working through my anger, I finally just felt sad and hopeless. Why was this happening to me? What had I done to *deserve this? And why even try since nothing will work anyways.* Now I was moving from "persecutor" to "victim." As I moved into victim mode, I unconsciously began to view him as my "persecutor," and yes, I was *still* in the triangle!

How did I get out of the triangle? Stephanie and I realized that we were the problem, not him. By us doing more for him or working on his life more than he was, we were giving him a subtle but powerful message: "We don't believe you can make it on your own without us." Whether we believed this or not, it didn't matter—the message was being given by our actions. Our son even told Stephanie once, "Mom, stop being the Creative Director of my life." Ouch! This made us do an unusual thing—to let our son live his own life! We told him that we were inviting him to experience total independence from us. It was a risk but it was the best thing for him and for us. And what happened? He found a great place downtown, moved in with all he owned, and rose to the occasion. By releasing him, we were giving him the spoken and unspoken message that we *believed* he could do it—and he did it. Not only did he become more confident and independent, we became healthier, less stressed, and we all were much happier. Our relationship drastically improved. He has since found healthy ways to overcome anxiety and depression, and he's created the life he wants as a professional musician. Music has been a powerful therapy for him.

Stepping out of the trauma-drama triangle isn't easy, but it is necessary—

necessary for your mental health and necessary for the emotional growth of the person you are trying to help. A simple model to stay out of the triangle requires a person to change:

from being a victim to becoming creator;

from being a rescuer to becoming a coach;

from being a persecutor to becoming a challenger.

While a victim says "poor me," a creator is aware that there are always choices in life. To the best of your ability, you can create the life you want. A creator knows that what we believe and assume helps to create our reality and experience. While a victim focuses on how to get rid of problems, a creator focuses on envisioned outcomes; in other words, they imagine what kind of life they would like to have or what kind of person they would like to be. Instead of solving one temporary problem after the next, attention is given to small steps that can be taken to move towards outcomes that are satisfying and sustainable. A creator realizes that they were made in God's image, the most creative being, and makes choices for his or her own life that will be fulfilling and rewarding.

We have seen this with one of our Courage girls in Africa. "Deborah" had been at Courage House in Tanzania for three years; she had been terribly abused in her past and had feelings of worthlessness. She struggled in school and failed her national exams twice. She was so discouraged and you could see her self-esteem was very low. She started treating the staff and girls badly, and we almost needed to ask her to leave Courage House. Last year, we were meeting with her and she looked at me (Stephanie) and said, "Mama, I am not going to let you down. I promise...you'll see." She became resolved, changed her attitude and focus, and we've seen incredible growth in her this past year. She worked hard in school and gained a new confidence. She was tender and kind to her sisters, respectful and helpful to the staff, and she has been a good leader. We are so proud of her! She's taken charge of her life and future and graduated from Form 4 (high school). She is doing well in college and will graduate this year. She has dreams of teaching children and we'd love to hire her at Courage House if she continues on the right path. What a change! But it started with her resolve to overcome her past, create the life she wants, and make right choices for her future.

While a rescuer says "they need me," a coach sees others as creators. While not denying a person's past, a coach encourages others to focus on the future and create their own solutions. While a rescuer throws their energy and resources at solving the person's problem, a coach directs their energy and resources at developing the person. Whereas a rescuer will tend to make plans, decisions, and arrangements for a victim, a coach asks questions that challenge and empower, such as, "What would you like to do?" "What would you like your life to look like?" and so on. Just as in any sport, the coach is not the player—the coach can encourage, question, train, strategize, and motivate, but they cannot go on the field. Ultimately, the player(s) decide the outcome of the game.

We were teaching with another local NGO who works with children in Tanzania. One of the staff members told us the light bulb went on for her with this teaching. She said to us, "You know, in Tanzania we are born in the triangle!" She realized she had been the rescuer with her adult brother who needed medical attention monthly. She would send him money every month so that he could travel to the clinic and take care of his problem. She decided that he was capable of taking care of himself. So she called him and told him this, "I know you can do it and figure this out... it's time you take care of yourself. You can do it." He was surprised, but he figured it out. He decided to move closer to the clinic to save on the transport costs and he's been taking care of himself ever since. Now he is empowered and she has a little more money for her needs every month! When she reported back to us, she was so excited about these changes.

While a perpetrator says, "I will hurt those who hurt me," a challenger sees the potentially constructive passion that is behind the perpetrator's anger. Rather than anger, revenge, or control, a challenger seeks to re-focus that negative energy into something positive. When a person is willing to forgive and learn from their pain, they can become a champion against injustice and fight for others who are marginalized and hurting.

When Jenny Williamson heard that children were being sold for sex, at first her heart was broken, but then it turned to anger. She was angry that this was happening and the resources weren't there to help care for these children. She channeled the anger into doing something positive; and instead of complaining or protesting, she decided she would build them a home and call them family. That is how Courage House was started.

After much favor, growth, and success in the battle against sex trafficking and caring for children who are victims, Courage Worldwide went through a difficult season when a local newspaper was informed of some internal struggles the organization was having. Negative articles based on interviews from a few disgruntled employees were published. It was frustrating because the articles were biased and based on sensational reporting with a lot of misinformation. Stephanie wrote a letter to the editor, which they didn't publish, but it explained why this was happening and how the "Trauma-Drama Triangle" related to it.

This was her post on Facebook, which we realized resonated with people since it had over 130 shares and many comments:

"For those who may want to hear my perspective, I wrote a letter to the editor in response to the negative articles about the non-profit I work for. The editor has not responded or been interested in printing the full story. They also did not correct the misinformation in the articles when it was brought to their attention. (Please feel free to share as the truth needs to be known.)"

September 21, 2016

Dear editor,

I am writing to give you another Courage Worldwide employee's perspective on our organization, our leadership, our girls and the battle we have taken on these last 8 years to provide care for minor children that have been so terribly traumatized. There is a whole other side to the story that I feel you and your readers need to know about.

Interestingly enough, I first met Jenny Williamson in August of 2008, when I saw a front-page article exposing the issue of sex trafficking of children in our own community and Jenny's dream to build Courage House. After meeting Jenny, I volunteered to put on benefit concerts, do 2 CD's with local and national musicians and was eventually hired as Creative Director. I was also a chaplain/mentor to our girls at Courage House and I am now the Community Relations and Resource Director. I have a unique perspective having worked on the corporate side of Courage Worldwide and also at Courage House with the girls and staff.

Before we found a good trauma therapist, Jenny and I were some of the first people our girls processed their stories with. The hideous details of their trauma gave me nightmares and I shed many tears. I never imagined such evil could be done to children, even though I myself was a victim of 2 sexual assaults in my teen years. I know what it took to overcome that trauma.... our girls who are victims of sex trafficking have been abused and raped thousands of times so their healing journey is a long road. I also testified at age 19 against my attacker —something that 2 of our girls did successfully. Their courageous testimonies put their attacker and trafficker away for many years.

We've had many incredible staff and volunteers come and go through the years at Courage House. The work is difficult and often draining. The trauma of our girls is extreme - they have PTSD where disassociation, flashbacks and violent outbursts are the norm. I've personally had my hair pulled, been cussed out, spit on and some of our staff have had their lives threatened. It is common for some of our girls to love us one minute then hate us the next depending on the day. It tests even the strongest of people. It's been difficult to find emotionally healthy staff to work with our population. You see, many people who want to get involved in this line of work often have their own story and haven't gone fully through their own healing process.

The most challenging part of our work is keeping everyone on the same page. When our girls come to Courage House, they come with a team of social workers, lawyers, judges, probation officers, counselors, CASA workers and more. Then they come to Courage House and they now have our treatment team – another therapist, social worker, administrator, chaplain, teacher, and executive director. In addition, we have line staff who often become like a sister, aunt or "mama" to our girls as well as volunteers and mentors. There are often many strong opinions about what is best for the girls and it is a challenge for all to come into agreement.

In my 30 years of church and non-profit work, I have never seen such extreme dynamics between people in an organization. Our organization has high standards and hires staff who are not only qualified, but who love our girls and believe wholeheartedly in the vision of Courage Worldwide. The trauma of the girls can also bring secondary trauma even to the best of us. We've all experienced it. There can be a love/hate relationship our girls have with each other, or with staff... then at times we have staff or volunteers who "turn" on each other. This all goes beyond the normal conflict in a work environment. Just this year, our trauma experts, Dr. Vanessa Snyder and Dr. Benjamin Keyes, explained to us that this dynamic is called the Trauma-Drama Triangle and it is a normal part of what they see in their work with trauma victims as well as organizations that work with trauma *victims. This "revelation" has helped us recently understand this dynamic and now we know how to better train, process and respond to it.*

I have with worked closely with Jenny Williamson since I met her 8 years ago and she is a bold and humble leader with a clear vision. She's never claimed to have all the answers or that she's qualified for this job. She's done this work because it's been her calling, and she'll be the first to admit when she's wrong and seek out a better way, all with the girls' ultimate best in mind. The girls have never been exploited by her or by our organization. Jenny is very protective of them - even turning down national media requests for interviews of our girls.

I've seen her give much grace to our staff and volunteers and create a culture of honor. It's been vital to protect the unity of our team, so there is direct and what we call "fierce" conversations at times. No one has ever been fired randomly. Good and dedicated employees have stuck with Courage Worldwide and been committed through the ups and downs over the years and corporate staff, including Jenny, have taken the "hits" with financial pay-cuts and lay-offs so that our staff at Courage House wouldn't have to. It's very interesting and disappointing that you only interviewed disgruntled former employees when there are many of us who have been around for years.

Here's the most important reality to keep in mind - we have had over 350 calls for placement for girls in the Sacramento region, some as young as 8 and 10 years old and we had to turn them away for lack of beds. We've worked with over 65 girls the last 5 years at our Courage Houses. We have very good outcomes with this population that few organizations have. Many of our girls are now thriving and living in freedom from their life of exploitation - some have transitioned to families, are going to college or vocational school, are working jobs, are raising children and some are in the military. The reality is also that some of our girls struggle as they transition from Courage House and go back to their communities and/or families and we are here for them when they want help. The journey of recovery and healing for our girls is long and hard and we're in for the long haul to support them in their dreams the best that we can.

I can honestly say that our employees, past and present at Courage Worldwide, have done the best they can with what they know in the midst of great challenges. Have we been perfect? No. But like I recently told one of the first girls who came to Courage House, you were loved like family. Family is not perfect - ever. Family makes mistakes and has conflicts, but we live, love, do our best to forgive and learn through it all. We will not give up or quit and we will continue to fight for all of the girls who need Courage House.

That's what family does.

Sincerely,
Stephanie Midthun
Community Relations Director, Courage Worldwide

How to Avoid the Triangle

Some questions you can ask yourself in order to avoid the triangle are:

- What is my motive for helping this person?
- Are my efforts to help given freely or are they tied to some particular outcome?
- Am I working harder on someone else's life and healing than they are willing to work?

Galatians 6 has some good advice for those of us who are natural rescuers:

"Brothers, if someone is caught in a sin, you who are spiritual should restore him gently. But watch yourself, or you also may be tempted. *Carry each other's burdens*, and in this way you will fulfill the law of Christ. If anyone thinks he is something when he is nothing, he deceives himself. Each one should test his own actions. Then he can take pride in himself, without comparing himself to somebody else, *for each one should carry his own load.*" (Galatians 6:1–5, emphasis mine)

We are to help carry each other's burdens and consequences of sin without judgment or comparison. But do you notice anything about verse 2 and verse 5? We are to carry each other's burdens but each one should carry his own load...

so which is it? Well, as with many biblical ideas, both are true, and it is usually a question of timing and nuance to help us live it out completely. There are two different words used for "burden" in verse 2 and "load" in verse 5.

"Burden" has an aspect of heaviness attached to it and is the idea of one person helping another with a heavy weight that is too much for one person. There are times and situations in a person's life that are too much for them to handle; there are times when we must step into another's life and help them carry it. It means to carry the burden with them, not for them. They must be willing to help carry it too. In other words, don't work harder on someone's healing than they are working. Of course, there are situations when we will carry their burden alone if they are physically or mentally incapable, but these are the exception, not the rule.

"Load" has the sense of a job or responsibility that is assigned to a person. It is different for each person depending on their capacity and ability, and it is expected that they will carry this themselves. When we step in to carry things that are meant to be that person's responsibility, we can enable them. When we let them carry these things themselves, we empower them.

While at times we may feel that we have lost the battle, we can win the war by not quitting. What makes us want to quit? When unexpected challenges come our way. When our disappointments begin to chip away at our faith in God's goodness and faithfulness. When we get stuck in the trauma-drama triangle and it slowly and silently sucks the life and joy out of us.

Coming to the realization that you are affected by things outside your control is a very freeing thing. Knowing that you are in the triangle and that you can choose to exit is very empowering. Discovering healthier ways to relate to others saves your time, your energy, and your sanity so that you can sustain the calling of God on your life.

Song Story: Shalom

As most parents know, sometimes we can be anxious about how our kids will turn out when they grow up. We can also feel guilt that we aren't doing this parenting thing right and that we are messing up our kids.

One day, I was feeling especially anxious about my young teenage son after his teacher called to share a few concerns. The worry in my heart just kept growing as the day went on. My mind started racing with all the "what-if's."

What if we've messed up? What if he goes off the deep end? What if he ends up in jail? What if, what if, what if....?

I decided to stop, pray, and seek God for my sanity and my son's well-being, and I found a great verse in the Bible:

> "You will keep in *perfect peace*, him whose mind is steadfast, because he trusts in You." (Isaiah 26:2)

This is what I needed—*perfect peace* or "shalom," which means *wholeness in mind, body, and soul.* As I was reflecting on this Scripture, I started hearing a melody and went to the piano and wrote the song "Shalom" in less than an hour.

I'll never forget that day—I would go and sing *Shalom* and then a few minutes later start feeling anxious again. Then I'd go back to the piano and sing it again, feeling such peace, only to have the anxiety return moments later. I must have sung that song at least twenty times that day. I remember my son having enough of hearing the song and yelling, *"Mom, can you please stop?!"* I wanted to yell back, *"It's because of you that I keep singing this,"* but I restrained myself!

"Shalom"

By Stephanie Midthun

(ISAIAH 26:2)

You will keep in perfect peace
When my mind is steadfast
Because I trust in You

You establish peace for me
All I have accomplished
You have done for me

Open the gates that the righteous may enter
Open the gates for the nations with faith
Open the gates that the righteous may enter
Open the gates of the nations with faith

I will trust in You Lord forever
You are my rock eternal
I will trust in You Lord forever
You are my hope righteous Father.

REFLECTION QUESTIONS

1. What stood out to you in this chapter?

2. Have you been caught up in the Trauma-Drama Triangle before? Are you now? How can you get out? Read Galatians 6:1–6; how does it speak to your current situation?

3. Do you feel like quitting? Do you want to give up? Ask God if He is releasing you or if you need to be strengthened to persevere through this season.

4. Read and memorize Isaiah 26:2 and allow God's shalom, His perfect peace to fill your heart each day.

7.

Emotional Health

Not again, Lord...

DO YOU EVER FEEL THAT WAY WHENEVER YOU HEAR ABOUT ANOTHER corrupt leader, fallen pastor, church split, dysfunctional missionary, or financial mismanagement of a ministry?

The truth is that we cannot separate our spiritual growth from our emotional maturity. Could this be why so many Christians are seeking holiness but lack emotional wholeness, and why so many are seeking spiritual gifts but lack the gifts of the Spirit from Galatians 5:22–23 (love, joy, peace, patience, and so on)?

There are so many highly-passionate, incredibly-gifted, and powerfully-anointed Christians who are terribly emotionally unhealthy. They can be self-centered, unable to deal with conflict, manipulative, passive-aggressive, and have very little self-control in their life.

These are people who you might listen to and perhaps want prayer from, but whom you wouldn't enjoy working with or hanging out with. How can this be? They love God, have the Holy Spirit living in them, and are committed to serving God, even sometimes sacrificing to follow His call.

A few years ago, we became aware of a book that has been a game-changer for us called *Emotionally Healthy Spirituality* by Peter Scazzero. He quotes,

> *"I was a Christian for twenty-two years, but instead of being a twenty-two-year-old Christian, I was a one-year-old Christian twenty-two times. I kept doing the same things over and over again." ~ Longtime Christian[5]*

The truth is that, while many Christian leaders are very gifted, many of them are not emotionally healthy. One of our closest mentors over the years, Pastor Mike Bradley, is one of the healthiest leaders we know. He leads with confidence but has no need to be in charge; he is never in a hurry, and he always makes you feel as though you are the most important thing on his agenda. We learned the following teachings from Mike (based on the leadership teachings of Pastor Jim Anderson, theharborchurch.com).

When Mike does leadership training, he asks the question: What are the consequences if church leaders aren't emotionally mature? One significant result is the high turnover of leadership in churches and ministries. In the United States, only 1 out of 10 pastors retires as a pastor. Significant causes of their career change stem from:

- Burnout
- Moral failure
- Divorce
- Church split
- Shame-based teaching and manipulation
- Unhealthy ways of dealing with conflict (passive-aggressive)
- Lack of healthy boundaries (personal and professional)

So how does this happen? How do good pastors and leaders start out with so much passion and love, yet end up five to twenty years later numb and burned-out? One way to see how this happens is illustrated by what is called the "Wall of Ministry Strength."

When you have success on higher levels, it puts more pressure on the layer beneath it. The greater your gifting or skills, the more pressure on your character and integrity. For instance, a very gifted preacher who is pastoring a fast-growing mega-church is under incredible pressure—both from the high praises and increased criticisms they will receive. This pressure puts a tremendous amount of weight on the unseen part of their life. If the lower layers of character and wholeness are not healthy, it will be only a matter of time before this leader's life, and ministry shows cracks and begins to crumble.

And it's not just pastors of large churches who suffer. Pastors and leaders of smaller ministries are also under considerable pressure to grow, to be more successful, and raise more finances. They also tend to have closer relationships with their people, so the stress and conflicts that come up can be more personal and more painful.

A leader's strength of character is directly connected to their level of emotional wholeness. When a person's wholeness and identity is not primarily built on the unconditional and unchanging love of God, the ups and downs of life and ministry will slowly erode, testing their emotional wholeness until it finally cannot stand any longer.

The Wall of Ministry Strength

So how does this happen? One helpful way to see how this works is demonstrated by what we call the "Wall of Ministry Strength." Success on each level brings great pressure on the layer beneath. If the lower layers of character and wholeness are not strong enough, it will be only a matter of time before it all crumbles. The greater the gifting a person has, the more success they could have, but also the greater the test and weight will be put on their character and wholeness. When a person's identity is not based on the unconditional love of God, the ups and downs of life will slowly erode and test their wholeness until it finally cannot stand any longer.

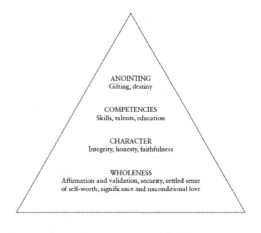

GOD AT WORK

The lack of emotional and spiritual wholeness is an important issue, because if God does not fill these wounds with His healing touch, then some of the consequences may be:

- Work and ministry dysfunction;
- Wounds that the enemy (devil) will feed on (Eph. 4:27);
- Wounded pride, division, and bitterness;
- Self-medicating through substance abuse, sinful habits, or illegitimate relationships;
- An identity tied to ministry success or failure, burnout.

On the other hand, when we allow the Holy Spirit to heal and change us, we become more mature and healthier. These are some characteristics of healthy people:

- Differentiation: the ability to be you and let others be himself or herself without detaching, criticizing, controlling, or manipulating;

- The ability to be un-offended (like Jesus) no matter what others say or do to you;

- The ability to share your weaknesses and accept constructive criticism in a way that makes you better and stronger;

- The ability to have difficult conversations with grace and truth;

- Servant leadership: leading in a way that serves those under your authority and raises them to their highest potential (Matt. 20:26).

The higher our anointing or gifting, the healthier we need to be emotionally. Only when our identity in Christ is sure, do we have a strong enough foundation to hold the weight of high levels of anointing or gifting.

Shame: The Raincoat of the Soul

We have learned much about shame from friend and fellow pastor, Dr. Robert Walter, who teaches often on the subject in the U.S., in Asia, and India. He has some great resources at www.ongodstrail.com.

Dr. Walter's book, *If I'm Forgiven, Why Do I Feel so Bad?* says that shame is a huge issue when it comes to emotional health. While guilt says, "I did something wrong," shame says, "I am wrong." Shame is so toxic because it is related to our identity rather than our actions. Shame can be experienced because of the things we do, but also it can be put on us through the negative words or abusive actions of others. Shame is something that is very difficult to get rid of...one description of shame is the "raincoat of the soul." While it can be helpful for us to feel appropriate shame about certain things we have done, toxic shame is tied to who we are. Rather than change our bad behavior, toxic shame keeps us in an unhealthy cycle by encouraging us to hide, convincing us that our behavior cannot change because it is who we are.

When we feel shame, we can react in different ways: We can hide from others, or we can attack others, or we can blame others. Shame can also lead us to hate ourselves.[6]

It was revelatory that girls who have been trafficked probably carry the most shame of any other population. According to studies, the four groups of people who experience the most shame in the world are (in order): women, minorities, criminals, and victims of abuse. In most cases, the girls who come to Courage House in the U.S. and Africa fit all or most of these groups.

Although shame is mentioned more times in the Bible (over 300 times) than guilt (over 150 times), those of us from the West focus on the power of the cross to remove guilt rather than its power to remove shame. This is due to cultural rather than theological reasons. There are "Guilt/Innocence" cultures based on laws and justice (U.S.A. and Europe), "Shame/Honor" cultures based on relationships and reputation (Asia and Africa), and "Power/Fear" cultures based on fear of retribution (Africa/New Guinea, etc.). (More detailed information on this can be found at www.shamehonor.com.)

Understanding these concepts can help those of us in the West make more sense of the world. For instance, it does not make sense to us that a young man would strap a bomb to himself and blow himself to bits just to make a religious point. But in the shame/honor context, it is easier to see why someone would value "honoring" (in their mind) their religion or God even over their own life.

This is useful when we read the Bible, because if we understand that the Israelites in the Old Testament era, and Jesus and the New Testament writers, lived in a Shame/Honor collectivistic culture, then we can know that their main goal in life was to avoid shame, acquire honor, and keep good relationship with the community. Sin is wrong primarily because it brings shame to God and to His people and breaks relationship with Him (covenant). In a way, Jesus's whole life can be viewed as a walk of shame. From a shameful birth out of wedlock, to being uneducated, poor, from the hick town of Nazareth, to the most shameful death—being hung on a tree. All of his life was lived to bring glory (honor) to his Father (John 12:28; 14:13).

So we have to ask, how is shame affecting or limiting you? I know that shame has affected me (Joel) and still does from time to time. It is the feeling I get when I don't feel skilled or qualified enough to do something. It is the voice that says, "Who do you think you are to try and do _____?" "*You're too quiet to make a difference.*" Or, "*You are too fearful to do great things.*"

Shame is a silent killer, and it must be identified before it can be dealt with. It can be helpful to name your shame by completing the sentence:

I'm not _____ enough.

I'm not strong enough, smart enough, educated enough, pure enough, and so on...

It can be anything that you use to disqualify yourself or feel worthless and rejected.

The good news is that Jesus came to free us from shame. As a faithful son who honored his Father, he takes on our shame and the negative consequences of it, which is separation from his Father. This is why he screamed, "Why have you forsaken me!" while he was on the cross. And why Paul and Peter both declared, "No one who believes in Him will be put to shame" (Rom.10:13; 1 Pet. 2:6).

Not only does Christ remove our shame, he also restores our honor. Jesus said, "I have given them the glory that you have given me" (John 17:22; Rom. 2:10). Believers will be glorified and honored with Jesus (2 Thess. 1:12, 2:14). This is why the Bible uses phrases like, "God's chosen people," "body of Christ," "now you are my friends," and "spirit of adoption." God is in the business of taking our shame and restoring our honor; that is, our value in the community of believers and our relationship to the family of God.

SONG STORY: DESPERATE

My sister, Carolyn, wrote this beautiful song after a time spent before the Lord in prayer and repentance for areas she wanted to change. She felt a deep desperation for the presence of the Lord in her life and this song flowed out of that cry. She grabbed a piece of paper and literally wrote the song while on her face before the Lord. It's very powerful and one of my all-time favorite songs we sing together as sisters.

"Desperate"

By Carolyn Cain

(PHILIPPIANS 3:10; 1 CORINTHIANS 13:12)

Lord I need Your presence
My sin is ever before me
I need Your holiness to surround me
I see you in a mirror dimly
But I want to see you more clearly
I need to feel your heartbeat
Lord I'm desperate for You
I'm longing for You
Deep within my soul
I want to know You more and more
On my face before You
Now yearning for more

Open the window of heaven
For a glimpse of Your glory
I'm not satisfied with complacency
I want more of You Lord and less of me
I need Your holiness to overwhelm me
Jesus purify me and help me see
That without you Lord I am nothing
I need to feel your heartbeat

REFLECTION QUESTIONS

1. Take the Emotional Health Test online at www.emotionallyhealthy. org. You just need to put your first name, last name, and email. It is very easy to take the test. Allow about thirty minutes.

2. Reflect on your test results and the areas you need to grow (emotional infant, emotional child, emotional adolescent, or emotional adult); discuss it with a trustworthy person in your life.

3. How do you usually react to shame (hiding, blaming, or attacking)? Reflect on Genesis 3 and 4 and how Adam, Eve, and Cain reacted to shame.

8.

Rest Is Your Greatest Weapon

MANY TIMES, I (JOEL) HAVE WOKEN UP IN THE MORNING AND NOT WANTED to get up. But only once have I woken up and been *unable* to get up. It was a cold, grey, Northern California, January morning, and the day I was to leave for a fun and encouraging retreat with a group of good pastor friends in the sun and sand of a beach city in Southern California. Despite being all packed and having a plane ticket and wanting to go, I couldn't. I had never felt so tired and exhausted in my body, mind, and spirit. As my wife stared at me in disbelief, I sheepishly tried to explain that I couldn't get up, had to cancel my trip, and had no rational reason why.

As I lay there for a few days, I heard God say one thing to me:

"Without me you can do nothing!"

Was I trying to live life and do ministry without God, even though I was a pastor? I thought about my past year of life. Had I trusted God? Yes. Had I prayed and sought God? Yes. Had I invited the Holy Spirit to work? Yes. What hadn't I done? Slowly, the answer came...rest. Although I had a regular day off, I still was not at rest in my spirit. On the outside I was confident, fairly successful, and relaxed, but on the inside, I was often worried, anxious, frustrated, discouraged, and weighed down by the things of family life and ministry.

REMEMBER THE SABBATH AND KEEP IT HOLY

This is the most broken commandment, the least followed; and pastors and those in helping professions are the worst offenders. This could be why only 1 in 10 pastors retire as a pastor. The reasons are legion: falling into sin, falling into depression, physical health issues, being let go, church conflict, financial problems, and toxic relationships, to name a few.

African pastors even have a saying to justify themselves, "We will rest when we get to heaven." That is why when I do trainings for African pastors I now tell them, "If you don't rest, you will get to heaven sooner!"

In the Tanzanian Lutheran churches, Mondays are their scheduled day off, but that is also the day most people visit them and schedule their weddings and funerals. Why? Because that is the day their church members can be sure they are available! How much of our struggles in life and ministry are because we break the Sabbath on a regular basis? In Ezekiel 20, one of the reasons given for the exile of the Jews from Israel into Babylon was for breaking the Sabbath.

Also with uplifted hand I swore to them in the desert that I would disperse them among the nations and scatter them through the countries, because they had not obeyed my laws but had rejected my decrees and desecrated my Sabbaths, and their eyes lusted after their fathers' idols. (Ezekiel 20:23–24)

Some theologians have suggested that the seventy years Israel spent in exile was one year for every seventh year of rest that had not been taken in the Promised Land (every seventh year was to rest the people and the land, a total of 490 years).

My stepdad, Dale, is a very spiritual and intelligent man. He has taught an adult Sunday school class at his church for over fifty-five years. He was also a math professor at Hamline University for his entire career and he wrote over ten mathematics textbooks. Yes, he is the guy who writes all the problem sets that students must solve! Earning a PhD in mathematics was very demanding. While his graduate student colleagues studied every day, including Sunday, Dale was committed to taking Sunday as his Sabbath for rest and worship. He followed the rule, "no studying on Sunday." How did this help? Dale finished his PhD on the regular schedule. Two of his closest colleagues were delayed by mental breakdowns, and another never did finish the PhD program.

Dale also is a committed giver, tithing at least ten percent of his income to his church and Christian missions. When asked by his publisher to write a major calculus book with the promise of large royalties, Dale and his wife made this a subject of extended prayer. They both came to peace after they agreed to give ninety percent of any royalties to Christian missions. Does it surprise you to learn that the resulting calculus book produced more income than all the other textbooks combined that Dale wrote? The calculus book was used at over one hundred colleges. This included schools such as the University of Chicago, Saint Olaf College, Wheaton College, Rutgers University, and The Ohio State University.

Taking a Sabbath and resting is, in a way, a tithing of our time. Trusting that God can do more with six days of our work than we can do with seven days of our work takes faith. Taking a Sabbath is how we "restore our soul," and it is a way to enjoy God and His creation. A way to connect with God and be reminded that He is eternal and we are finite is to stay faithful to the Sabbath—rest.

In Matthew 11:30, Jesus says, *"My yoke is easy and my burden is light." On the other hand, when we take on our own yoke, life is hard and heavy.* "

Hebrews 4:9–11 says, *"There remains, then, a Sabbath rest for the people of God; for anyone who enters God's rest also rests from his own work, just as God did from his. Let us, therefore, make every effort to enter that rest, so that no one will fall by following their example of disobedience."* We must work at rest. Yes, that is right, "make every effort to enter that rest."

What Is the Purpose of a True Sabbath?

Enjoying God and His creation, meaning that recreation is re-creation. Worshipping God corporately is an essential part of rest and renewal. Weekly corporate worship keeps us connected to the body of Christ, to the Word of God, and to the Holy Spirit. Enjoying (receiving joy in) what we love to do, hiking, music, books, exercise, and friends, connects us to the true center of God's love and joy.

Resting in God's sovereignty means releasing outcomes to God. Taking a day (or a 24-hour period) reminds us how small we are and how big God is. It forces us to stop working, thinking, and scheming, and to rest in his plans and timing.

Expecting God's provision means tithing your time. How can we rest when we are lacking time or resources? Tithe one-seventh of your time believing that God will multiply your time, money, and effectiveness.

Renewing God's people results in becoming more productive. God created a system for humans to live in, that is, resting one day in seven. Breaking this natural law causes strife, mistakes, sickness, stress, and other unnecessary pain. Taking advantage of this blessing brings fresh ideas, new energy, and a higher perspective.

Peter Scazzero tells us, "Henry Ford, in the mid-1920s, the auto giant, reduced his factories' workweek from six days to five, and 48 hours to 40, after discovering that productivity returns diminished steadily after his workers toiled eight hours a day, five days a week." [7]

Many people take time to plan their Sabbath by getting chores and other necessary things done the day before so that their Sabbath does not get stolen or watered down. Just be careful not to make your Sabbath day too legalistic like the Pharisees did—keep it simple and just enjoy it.

Song Story: Rest

We had just started Living Water Church in 1999. I was in my early 30's, our sons were young, and my sisters and I decided to record our first worship album. It was an exciting time in our lives, and I love doing new things! I was in the prime of my life, our church was growing, and I loved starting this music ministry with my sisters. Life was good. Since the three of us were spread throughout California, it was fun to be together, and there's nothing better than the harmonies of sisters—we have always loved singing together for fun but didn't get to do this much except for holidays.

Soon after we finished our acoustic worship recording, I started having some unusual symptoms—numbness in my hands and face, as well as extreme fatigue. Even though I was so tired and fatigued, I wouldn't sleep well at night. I kept thinking I was imagining things, but it just kept getting worse as the days went on. I didn't feel stressed at the time, so I knew the insomnia wasn't from that.

I researched my symptoms and got worried when I saw that these symptoms could be an indication of Multiple Sclerosis (MS). I went to the doctor and she sent me to a neurologist for testing. I heard nothing on results for weeks, which stretched out to months.

Although I was a little nervous about it, I tried a chiropractor and I'll never forget what he said to me: "Stephanie, you better hope I can help you, otherwise it's probably a brain tumor, ALS (Lou Gehrig's Disease) or MS." I was stunned. Receiving this information did not help matters at all. What a quack! (No offense to the good chiropractors out there!)

The waiting game was intense—days turned into weeks and weeks into months, and still no word as to what I was suffering from.

I had no energy most days and just doing laundry would reduce me to tears. I felt so bad that Joel had double duty, not only pastoring our new church plant but doing most of the housework, yard work, and caring for our boys. I was bedridden about half the time—the other half I was too wiped out to accomplish much. I still led worship at our church but found myself sneaking out early to avoid talking with people, which took energy that I didn't have.

The sleeplessness continued and one night all I could see in my mind was a picture of a woman I knew who was in a wheelchair from MS, had young children, and eventually passed away. I cried out to the Lord… I couldn't imagine dealing with this. What would happen to my kids and Joel?

I was up late one sleepless night and started reading these verses:

"This then, is how we know that we belong to the truth, and how we set our hearts at rest in His presence whenever our hearts condemn us. For God is greater than our hearts and He knows everything." (1 John 3:19–20, emphasis mine)

"There is no fear in love but perfect love drives out fear." (1 John 4:1)

"Come to me all you who are weary and heavy laden and I will give you rest." (Matt. 11:28a, emphasis mine

I prayed more and reflected on these verses. I read a powerful devotion by Oswald Chambers on suffering. I remember him saying, "Why should we not expect to suffer as a Christian when God bruised his very own son?" That night I surrendered it all to Him. No matter what was in my future regarding my health, I chose to believe and trust my Savior with my life and my family. I believed in healing and would still pursue that wholeheartedly but I decided to trust God in this season even if I wasn't healed.

I wrote the song "Rest" that night, and it became my anthem during those months of the unknown. It took six months to discover that I was suffering from an auto-immune disease called Chronic Fatigue Syndrome. It lasted for about two years in its acute stage, and I slowly recovered; but I must take enough time to rest my body and soul or I can easily relapse.

"Rest"

By Stephanie Midthun

Set our hearts at rest in Your presence
Whenever our hearts condemn us
Release the hold of sin
Restore to us again
The joy of knowing You

May Your perfect love come to us
And drive away our fear Lord Jesus
Draw near to us this day
Protect us Lord we pray
In Your Name
So we can rest

Set our hearts at rest
Set our hearts at rest
Set our hearts at rest
Set our hearts at rest

Come to me all you weary ones
And I will give you rest
Come to me and learn from me
And I will give you rest

REFLECTION QUESTIONS

1. Are there any ways that your identity is too closely tied to what you do (your ministry, job, or title)?

2. How is your health, relationships, or energy affected from lack of proper rest? How do you rest? Do you take a 24-hour Sabbath each week? Do you prioritize weekly corporate worship within a healthy Christian church?

3. How do your priorities or calendar need to change for you to be able to experience a real Sabbath each week?

9.

Walking in Authority

I (STEPHANIE) HAD A CAREER IN MUSIC MINISTRY IN THE CHURCH FOR about twenty-five years before God clearly called me into a job that was outside of the church walls. I started volunteering by performing concerts for Courage House and then eventually was hired as Creative Director for Courage Worldwide. Later I became the Community Resource Director, and it was a challenge for me. I needed to develop new skills in public speaking and often spoke at schools, clubs, business meetings, government meetings, and even the media, educating them on the sex trafficking of children and our mission. Sometimes I would be a bit overwhelmed, and I had to wrestle through my own insecurities of public speaking as God was stretching me and taking me to places and audiences I've never really connected with before. In a moment of weakness, I would say to my boss, Jenny, "I'm just a worship leader!" She would remind me, "Stephanie, THIS IS worship. You are going to the community and giving hope, inviting them to be a part of changing lives."

I realized she was right and that I am carrying the presence of God with me into the community, honoring Him, and bringing others into kingdom purposes—maybe without them even realizing it.

It was with a new and different level of authority and taking of new territory that God was calling me to walk. Now, I had *loved* church ministry, leading various choirs, putting on moving concerts, and leading worship. I loved bringing people into God's presence to connect with Him to bring healing and strength to their hearts. There was no greater joy for me than this.

But there was another defining moment for me. One of our Courage Ambassadors, Dawn Hershberger, who was a veteran correctional officer at a prison in Northern California, heard Jenny Williamson speak and God broke her heart for the children being trafficked. She just knew she had to do something. She worked tirelessly to get prison endorsements for our organization and to engage her fellow officers to make a difference. A fire was lit among them. I found that these courageous officers work with many of the perpetrators in prison, and it's a hopeless environment that they are in. There is so much recidivism with the inmates, and because of this, these officers can be hardened and cynical and feel that there is no hope for change. It's a super high-stress job as they work long hours and lay their lives on the line every day. Many have been attacked by inmates and nearly killed; some have even lost their lives. Others have committed suicide as there is a high rate of depression among them. I have so much respect for our law enforcement officers as they serve and protect our community every day. It's not easy.

Dawn invited us to a large gathering of law enforcement officers with top prison officials in attendance. Her hope was to engage them all in helping with fundraising for Courage Worldwide. She also wanted them to get a heart for the children who are victims so they could perhaps make a difference. I helped run a booth at this convention and one-by-one officers would come up and ask about what we were doing. At the last minute I got invited to speak for ten minutes, which was a huge honor even though I wasn't quite prepared. I admit I started to freak out. I hadn't really had time to prepare and I knew every word out of my mouth was important. One thousand law enforcement officers! Wow. How do I, *a pastor's wife* and *worship leader*, a churchy gal, connect with these men and women? My friend Charlene Carthen came with me to this convention and right before I spoke she prayed for me asking God to anoint my words. I felt a little shaky and had butterflies in my stomach.

But I'll never forget that moment.

They introduced me, and as I walked up the stairs to the stage, I suddenly felt the strong presence and power of God almost rush before me as I stepped up to the podium. I looked at these tough men and women who I had come to admire and appealed to their hearts as fathers and mothers. I told them briefly the horrors of what these children go through and said,

"What would you do if it was your daughter?"

You could hear a pin drop. I'm not sure what all I said after that, but after I finished, I had many come up to me who wanted to help. Big, strong, grown men had tears in their eyes. Some of the key officials approached me about how they can help with grants. I couldn't believe the response. Dawn and her team were so excited and she was in tears. She and her fellow officers now sponsor our Courage Triathlons, one of our most successful fundraising events, and they are making a big difference in the community. Even the inmates wanted to get involved, starting a "Not in My Life" campaign. They have been raising funds and educating other inmates. Who knew? That conference was one of the most powerful, anointed moments of my life. You see, God can use us in unexpected places if we just get out of the way, allow Him to fill us, and walk in boldness with the authority He gives.

I've reflected a lot on authority and boldness, but the importance of humility and laying down personal pride go along with it. Too many ministries or churches implode due to pride and insecurity among the leaders.

Boldness with humility is truly life giving. Insecurity and pride can bring death and destruction. We all need to check our hearts and deal with our insecurities. We all need that good friend to tell us the truth when we are off base. Sometimes pride can blind us as we all have blind spots; others can see our weakness but often we can't.

THE UPSIDE-DOWN KINGDOM

What is humility? Pastor Rick Warren famously wrote, "Humility is not thinking less of yourself, it is thinking of yourself less."[8] Jesus uses the word *meek* in the Sermon on the Mount to talk about humility (Matt. 5:5). Those with gentle strength will inherit the earth. Humility understands that the kingdom of God is an upside-down kingdom. It is a kingdom in which those who lead are servants, those who are weak are strong, those who are poor can be rich, and those who win must surrender.

A humble person not only mourns with those who mourn but also rejoices with those who rejoice (Rom. 12:15). It is painful to mourn with others and to feel their pain and take time with them. But it is often even harder to rejoice when others rejoice. Can you rejoice when someone gets married but you are single? When someone gets a raise but you don't? When someone's church or ministry is growing but yours isn't? This is the true test of humility.

It is so important to understand the difference between true humility and false humility. Scandinavians (which is our heritage) have an odd cultural dynamic called "the law of Jante," which we first heard about from Pastor Paul Anderson from Lutheran Renewal. This is an unwritten rule of thought that has a negative attitude toward individuality and success. It says, "don't think that you are better than us" or "that you are special or different." The Japanese say it this way, "the nail that sticks out is the one that gets hit." This is false-humility—thinking less of yourself than God thinks of you. We must remember that we are each made different and in God's image; we must learn to be secure enough in God's love that we can celebrate another's success without feeling slighted, jealous, or threatened. This is true humility.

Lead Us Boldly

My good friend Pastor Nathan Hoff (who is thoroughly Scandinavian), his wife Joy, and daughter Annika were captivated by Africa last year when they went for the first time. Though they were only there for nine days, they gave and received great impact with Lutheran pastors, leaders, and the girls at Courage House. As we were shown a two-acre property with three buildings that was for sale, Nathan exclaimed, "This would be perfect for Courage! How can we get it?" We gently explained to him that Courage was in a difficult financial season and had no money—and Nathan accepted this hard reality.

The following Sunday, Joy and Nathan shared in their own church about their trip and all that God did; they shared about the property that was available for $60,000 with no mention of fundraising. After church a woman handed Joy a check for $1,000 with the words, "Now you only have to raise $59,000." As Nathan met with his elder board Monday night, they all felt that God was calling them to raise the money, and it needed to be raised in one week. (We were returning to the U.S. shortly and we were the only ones who could handle such a transaction at that time.) After prayer, his elders told Nathan, "We need to do this, but lead us courageously, not cautiously."

One week later, we were on a Skype call with Nathan and Joy, counting down as the electronic gifts came in...$2,000 left, $1,500 left, $500 left. By 8:00 p.m. Pacific Time, one full hour before the deadline, 100% of the money was in! A few days later an additional $20,000 had been given. A week later we signed papers for the new Courage campus in Tanzania, a testament to a bold and humble leader's belief in a powerful and faithful God, and a church that not only believes but acts!

Before we left for Africa for a three-month sabbatical/mission trip, we wanted to encourage the leaders at our church to step up and lead with authority. We also wanted to encourage the whole church to step up during the three months that we were going to be away. On our last Sunday, we called up the elders and prayed for them, anointed them, and gave each of them a little bottle of oil, symbolizing their spiritual authority. We then called up all the church staff and volunteer leaders, and we joined the elders in praying for and anointing each of them. Finally, as all the leaders, staff, and elders were fanned around the front of the sanctuary, we invited each member of the congregation to come forward and receive prayer and anointing. The point is that we are *all* ministers in the kingdom of God. He has given *all* of us access to his authority—if we boldly and humbly use it.

African leaders, on the other hand, understand authority. In fact, sometimes they can lead with too much power and authority and not enough humility and servitude. For many of them, that is the model that was given to them by Colonialists and village chiefs—but Jesus has a better way.

SONG STORY: GOD, I BELIEVE

We were doing another benefit CD for Courage Worldwide in 2013 and Philip LaRue was producing several songs on the album. Cameron Stymeist and I worked to write a song for the Come Back Home album. I was always inspired by Jenny Williamson's faith and courage and wanted to write a song for this album that was inspired by her life message. She truly lives out her passion and message of living out her purpose by being a "water walker, a giant slayer, and a history maker!"

A couple of years ago, Cameron entered this song in an international songwriting competition where 25,000 songs were submitted, and it won first place in the Gospel category!

"God, I Believe"

By Cameron Stymeist and Stephanie Midthun

I need the strength to move these mountains

so calm the storms in me

I need the faith to walk on water

to live courageously

I need You, I need You, I need You to raise the dead in me

You're the reason I start singing

You put a song of hope in me

I find purpose in believing

and the freedom to be me

*my heart screams - my heart screams - my heart
screams, would You awaken me?*

God, I believe, but help these blind eyes see

God, I believe in You

May my weakness be Your strength

when I start to lose my way

Singing God, I believe in You

When the darkness clouds my vision

Give me power to overcome

I cry out the name of Jesus

and I know the battle's won

Be my hope, be my strength cause in You I can do anything!

BRIDGE

I find who I am in who You are

I find who I am in who You are

Copyright © 2013 Cam Style Music/ASCAP

REFLECTION QUESTIONS

1. Do you struggle more with stepping out in boldness or with staying humble?

2. How have you seen insecurity or pride tear down a good person or organization?

3. How have you seen lack of boldness hold back a person or organization?

4. Is pride an issue in your life? If you aren't sure, ask someone close to you. Oftentimes, we can have a blind spot in this area. Lay down pride and ask the Lord to clothe you with humility (1 Pet. 5:5).

10.

It Is Well with My Soul

"God wants to use a temporary trial to bring a permanent blessing."
~ Pastor John Bullock

THIS PAST SEASON HAS BEEN ONE OF THE MOST HEART-WRENCHING, confusing, and stressful seasons of our lives.

One of my (Stephanie) worst fears came true. For the last seven to eight years, we slowly lost my vibrant dad, who was only in his 60's, to a neuro-degenerative disease that stole everything from him; his dignity, ability to speak, read, sleep, travel, hunt, play music, and eventually feed or care for himself. My dad was a very strong man—a man's man. He was a pilot, hunter, outdoorsman, fitness buff, health nut, not to mention he became a wonderful husband, father, and grandfather. He was well loved and respected by many, a leader in his church who was known for going on mission trips and giving generously to missions and ministries.

No matter how hard we prayed and believed my dad would be healed, he continued to decline. It was like losing him ever so slowly and painfully. I still can't wrap my head around that long and painful season, one where I chose to trust God, but sometimes just didn't have words to pray. I would often just quietly weep and play the song "It Is Well" by Kristine Demarco on repeat. Other times I would just say out loud to myself, "It is well with my soul," even though my heart felt like it was breaking in two. It was also difficult to see the toll this took on my very strong mom who lovingly cared for my dad day and night for the past several years.

My beloved dad passed away October 19, 2016. My sisters and I sang at his funeral the songs that got me through losing my dad—"It Is Well with

My Soul," both the new Bethel song and the original hymn we love so much.

I'm reminded of the devastating loss from which the hymn was penned;

Horatio G. Spafford was a successful lawyer and businessman in Chicago, who lived with his wife Anna and five children. This family experienced their share of deep pain and loss as their young son died with pneumonia in 1871, and later that same year much of their business was lost in the great Chicago fire. On November 21, 1873, the French ocean liner, Ville du Havre was crossing the Atlantic with 313 passengers on board. Among the passengers were Mrs. Spafford and their four young daughters. Although Mr. Spafford had planned to go with the family, he had stayed home to deal with an unexpected business problem. He told his wife he would join her and their children in Europe a few days later.

About four days into the crossing of the Atlantic, the Ville du Harve collided with a powerful, iron-hulled Scottish ship, the Loch Earn. Suddenly all of those on board were in grave danger. Anna hurriedly brought her four daughters to the deck. She knelt there and prayed that God would spare them if that could be his will or make them willing to endure whatever awaited them. Within twelve minutes, the ship sank with 226 of the passengers, including the Spafford girls. A sailor rowing a small boat spotted Anna floating on a piece of the wreckage. She was still alive. Nine days later when she arrived on land, she wired her husband a message which began, *"Saved alone, what shall I do?"* (Mr. Spafford later framed the telegram and placed it at his office.) Mr. Spafford booked passage on the next available ship and left to join his grieving wife. With the ship about four days out, the captain called Spafford to his cabin and told him they were over the place where his children drowned. Spafford then penned the hymn "It Is Well with My Soul" while on this journey, which has touched many, many people over the years, even without knowing the story.[9]

But once you know why and how it was written, you can see why it is so anointed in deeply touching so many of our hearts.

"It Is Well with My Soul"

By Horracio S. Spafford and Phillip Bliss

When peace like a river attendeth my way
When sorrows like sea billows roll
Whatever my lot, Thou has taught me to say
It is well, it is well with my soul.

It is well, it is well
It is well, it is well with my soul.

Though Satan should buffet, though trials should come
Let this blest assurance control
That Christ has regarded my helpless estate
And hath shed His own blood for my soul

My sin, oh the bliss of this glorious thought!
My sin, not in part but the whole
Is nailed to the cross and I bear it no more
Praise the Lord, praise the Lord, oh my soul.

And Lord haste the day when my faith shall be sight
The clouds be rolled back as a scroll
The trump shall resound and the Lord shall descend,
Praise the Lord, praise the Lord oh my soul.

None of us will escape suffering loss and facing grief. But it is especially brutal when we lose a loved one prematurely. I (Joel) lost my dad when I was in my early 20's and my mom was only fifty-eight years old. I didn't quite know how to say goodbye to my dad. My mom wrote a powerful paper called "Graceful Conclusions" about loss. I have reprinted an excerpt she wrote about me and my dad.

> In the last days of Ernie's life, he was blessed by the good Word of the Lord, which was shaped to fit into the palm of his hand. In concluding this book, I want to tell about this good Word of the Lord. It is a true story about a dying father and his youngest son. It is a story of an Old Testament scripture that came ringing down through the centuries to the last days of a man called Ernie Midthun. I'd like to call it "A Midthun Moment of Abiding Astonishment."

> It came in the form of a small exquisite carving of a child's body carved into the palm of a hand, inspired by a verse from Isaiah.

> "Behold, I have carved you in the palm
> of my hand." (Isaiah 49:6)

> In our family, this little carving has become a God-given sign, a sign as tangible evidence of a spoken message, a sign as a miracle, something to wonder at!

> The little statue was carved by a Malagasy artisan who lived on an island 14,000 miles from our home in Minneapolis, where the dying father lay. That island called Madagascar, was very dear to Ernie's heart; it had been home to him and his family for 23 years. It was the birthplace of his three sons. When he left that land for the last time, he wept as grown men seldom weep.

> It is not easy to say goodbye. And now in his dying it was time for Ernie to say another goodbye. And it was time for us to say goodbye to Ernie. Many old friends and relatives had come to visit during those days and weeks of Ernie's dying. Between and through their reminiscing and laughter, their prayers and tears, Ernie could hear their unspoken farewells. "They came because I am dying," he said to his wife, and she could not deny it.

The visitor who walked into his room two days before his death was no chance visitor. She was one of Ernie's favorite people and her name was Pat. She had flown in from Madagascar the night before, and the next morning stepped into Ernie's room like a fresh breeze of the Indian Ocean. The nice thing about Pat was that wherever Pat was, she always remained Pat. She didn't change according to context or continent. A cancer ravaged body would not change Pat's reactions to the big man she knew as her friend Ernie.

They laughed and chatted together. Oh, the lovely sound of laughter in that somber time! She brought refreshing news of Madagascar and then out of the familiar Air France travel bag came a gift—the small statue. It was so light and easy to hold—shaped to fit into the palm of Ernie's hand, where it was to stay until later that evening. He found comfort in holding God's good Word so close, "Behold, I have carved you in the palm of my hand." He didn't tell me how precious it was to him, but the way he enclosed it in the palm of his hand said more than words could say.

But this was to be the story of a dying father and his youngest son. Where was the son during these days of "goodbyes," the beloved youngest son who for 20 years had been the "apple of his father's eyes"? Like a shadow, he was there in the house but alone in his grief; unable to talk about it or even believe it was happening.

This youngest son, Joel, had always had a passionate interest in God and his God was a BIG God. As a preschooler he had figured out just how big God was and told his parents, "God is so big that if he stood on Madagascar one foot would be in Africa."

With the help of four older siblings and his doting parents, Joel matured into a vibrant and talented young man. For two years he traveled around the United States singing, drumming and playing guitar with a Christian music witness team. His father was silently and inordinately proud of his son Joel.

While Joel was a student at the Lutheran Bible Institute in California, he attended Sunday night healing services at a charismatic church. His God was alive and powerful and able to heal. When Ernie was diagnosed with terminal cancer, Joel and his young friends prayed mightily and faithfully, believing that God could and would heal his father. The prayers of his sons and daughters were a great comfort to their father as cancer began to take its toll.

When Joel came home in June, it was obvious to him that his father really was dying. Joel spent hours by himself playing his guitar. Sometimes he played and sang for his father and mother, but he could not talk about the thing that was slowly and irrevocably changing their lives forever. "No man is an island," but I think Joel was an island that summer—alone and almost unnoticed.

Does the Holy Spirit give people a nudge? Why did Joel's mother stop him on the stairs that evening after Pat's visit and say, "Joel, please spend some time with your Dad tonight. He needs you. He needs to say goodbye to you and he needs you to let him go." When she glanced into the room a few minutes later, she saw that Joel had pulled a chair close to his father's bed and they were talking together.

When Joel came out of his father's room, there was a little bounce in his voice. "Yeah, Mom," he began. When Joel was in a happy mood, he often began a conversation this way. "Yeah, Mom. Dad and I had a nice talk. I told Dad I wasn't his little Joe anymore and that I would be okay no matter what happened."

And then came the small miracle—the sign to wonder at! Joel told me how his father held up the little carving from Madagascar and said, "I know you're not my little Joe anymore and I won't worry about you. You'll be okay without your old Dad around. You are God's child and he has carved you in the palm of his hand." Then he placed the small carving in the palm of Joel's hand. And Joel was comforted and blessed by the good Word of the Lord which was not beyond his reach but very near to him, in his heart and in his hand.

Ernie wasn't given physical healing but he was given spiritual healing, and God wasn't stingy. He gave this healing generously, not only to Ernie but also to his family and on this night to the youngest son Joel. And I now know that there can be "Graceful Conclusions" to life!

~ Louise Midthun Varberg

Betrayal and False Accusations

One of the hardest things to walk through is false accusation and betrayal. A friend of our family, who is a trauma therapist, said that betrayal is a deep trauma and not easy to heal from. We've faced some of this over the years, and our family did recently.

We came home from Tanzania after a month in March of 2017 to find that not only had our youngest son (who was in college) and his fiancé ended their engagement, but it ended with deep betrayal and ugly accusations. It was a nightmare for him and it broke our hearts to see how this betrayal deeply affected our son. Until this point, he had sailed through life with a strong faith and an inner confidence. He was musical and athletic and he was well loved by many people, a leader in about any area he chose to be, both at church and at school. We felt helpless and did everything in our power to help him through that season, praying that God would bring him through this battle and bring good and healing out of it all both for himself and his ex-fiancé. It seems at times that if the enemy can't get at us personally, then he goes after our children, which is even worse as a parent.

We also found our names and our church in the local paper. Distorted facts about us were printed in an article saying we had forced the Courage House girls to go to our church and exploited them. This couldn't be further from the truth. It also said we had "practiced religious rituals" on girls, when in fact they were prayed for and given Holy Communion when they requested it. The sensational reporting was ridiculous and hurtful.

This season tested our souls. We prayed a lot, had some sleepless nights, and asked the Lord to bring peace to these storms and strengthen us through them. The craziest thing was that throughout all these storms and battles, we felt a strong call to go full time to Tanzania, and each day it grew stronger.

"Are you sure we are hearing from you God? Can't we wait until all of this is settled down and we're on the other side? We need to make sure our son is okay, our church is okay, and CWW is okay and stable before we commit. Right?"

We both felt strongly that the Lord was saying, NOW is the time. I (Joel) heard God say one day,

"You don't get to wait for everything to be resolved, you just need to go."

Although the timing didn't make sense, we decided to trust God and be obedient. We told our family, sold our house (in three days!) and much of our belongings, announced the news to our leaders and beloved church of eighteen years, packed up most of our things all in three months' time, and here we are now in Tanzania, Africa.

Finances had been tough for the first few months here, and yet God had taught us something new... to be content in plenty and in want and realize *there is always enough*. Stephanie wrote this post on Facebook about it:

September 2017

There Is Always Enough.

Those words are echoing in my head tonight as I am reading this book about Heidi Baker and how God provided miraculously for their ministry in Africa. The Lord spoke to her and her husband early on when they were in times of desperation, "there's always enough." Now, over 20 years later they've helped thousands of orphans and planted thousands of churches and are having a massive global impact.

So often in ministry we see the needs and the lack of funds and can be anxious about how it's all going to work out. In the kingdom of God "there is always enough" when we are obedient to all God is calling us to do. He is a faithful and good Father!

Thirteen years ago, when I was first called to Africa, I was so overwhelmed and distraught by all the needs of street children and orphans I saw and how little resources I had to help. God told me to be His voice, His hands and feet, and just do my part and challenge others to do their part.

We are all called to do something to make an impact in this world and to make a difference.

Did you also need to hear this today for what you are called to do?

Love,

Steph and Joel

It was also during this season that we attended "Soul Camp" led by Pastor John Bullock and his wife, Debbie, along with a few missionaries here. John and Debbie talked about blockages in the soul and the things that keep us stuck from being transformed and not living an abundant life.

I, Stephanie, felt tears welling up as I thought of my dad and how he had transformed his life and lived so abundantly, yet the last years of his illness and death were so devastating. The Lord brought to the surface deep disappointment that had lodged itself in my soul because my prayers for my dad to be healed weren't answered. Unknowingly, disappointment had become a chain in my life and I realized it affected my believing God for healing and other miracles. My tears turned into sobs as I shared with our new friends; I received healing prayer for my broken heart. A new Australian friend, who was also a pastor's wife, prayed over me and shared this powerful picture with me…

> *"Stephanie, I saw Jesus on the cross, suffering from humili-ation, being mocked and misunderstood, losing all dignity. I heard him say that He went through all these things too and that He took it all for your dad. He took all of that pain and humiliation with him on the cross."*

I wept and wept and found this to be profoundly healing. Later, I shared it with my mom who found great comfort in this word too. She's been sharing it with others who've lost loved ones recently and said many of them were very touched.

And we are so grateful that our son Joshua is doing well. He switched colleges, has received counseling, and is thriving in his classes. We also like that he lives near his Grandma Carol, as it is a blessing for both. He is now excited about his future and has goals to become a doctor; and he is drawn towards missions! We know God has a great destiny for him and that He will bring good out of that difficult season in his life.

SLEEPING IN THE STORM

> *"You only have authority over the storm you can sleep in."*
> *~ Bill Johnson*

> *Now when they had left the multitude, they took Him along in the boat as He was. And other little boats were also with Him. And a great windstorm arose, and the waves beat into the boat, so that it was already filling. But He was in the stern, asleep on a pillow. And they awoke Him and said to Him, "Teacher, do you not care that we are perishing?" Then He arose and rebuked the wind, and said to the sea, "Peace, be still!" And the wind ceased and there was a great calm. But He said to them, "Why are you so fearful? How is it that you have no faith?" And they feared exceedingly, and said to one another, "Who can this be, that even the wind and the sea obey Him!" (Mark 4:36–41)*

During the middle of a storm that was stressing out seasoned fisherman, Jesus was taking a nap. When his anxious disciples woke him, he calmly took authority over the storm, released peace over it, and then expressed some surprise that the disciples didn't do it themselves. The same peace that Jesus had inside his spirit was now influencing the world around him. This shows us how the kingdom works and how faith works: it works from the inside-out, *and it works from a place of rest.*

Africa can be a scary place at night—there are no street lights, no 9-1-1 emergency services, the majority of people are home by dark and you feel sleepy far before 10:00 p.m. (the missionaries jokingly call 9:00 p.m. "Moshi Midnight" for a reason). Though we were sleeping alone on the second story of a house that was rented by a missionary friend, we felt very safe. The grounds are surrounded by an eight-foot wall, there is a guard on duty 24/7, and our metal front door gate was padlocked.

Imagine our surprise waking at 4:00 a.m. to loud pounding on our bedroom door, and yelling, "Stephanie and Joel! Are you there?? Are you okay?!" We recognized the voice of our good friend, Jill, who had lived in Tanzania for fifteen years—but how could she be in our *locked-up* house? She was relieved to hear us respond, "Jill, what is going on?"

We groggily dressed and walked downstairs only to meet a crowd of missionary friends and co-workers, and numerous police officers were walking around the property. We found that we had been robbed by several armed thieves who broke into our house. Word spread to our friends and staff, who had been trying to text and call us, and we slept through it all!

They feared the thieves had us and were hurting us. We were told that our security guard, who wasn't armed, hid as he saw these men dressed in black climb over the fence and break into our house. He texted the security company and they sent an armed guard. When he shot off his gun at the gate, the thieves all ran away. What had kept them from coming upstairs? There had been plenty of time for them to do so. We believe angels protected us as many people were praying for us. Although only one small blue-tooth speaker was taken, we shuddered to think of what could have happened. We were a bit shaken, but we both knew God had protected us. He had kept us in a deep sleep during this storm, He had kept the thieves from coming upstairs, and even though Stephanie woke briefly at 3:00 a.m. when she heard the dogs barking and almost went downstairs, she was too sleepy to get up!

It was a confirmation of God's goodness knowing that I had just written our first missionary newsletter earlier that same week on the topic of, you guessed it, "you only have authority over the storm you can sleep in." That morning, the sermon I had prepared to preach was from 2 Timothy 1:7, "For the Spirit God gave us does not make us timid, but gives us power, love and self-discipline."

Song Story: Heaven Is Our Home

As my (Stephanie) dad's dementia progressed, there were very few things he could truly enjoy anymore except for music. Sometimes when he was at his worst, we girls would take him to the piano and start to worship. He would then be engaged, raise his hands, close his eyes, and try to sing harmony with us, even though he couldn't follow the words. You could see he was taken away with the music in the presence of the Lord, and many times tears would stream down his face. This season taught me a lot. That the spirit is strong even though the body grows weaker and the mind fades. That this earth is not our home and that these trials are temporary. I wanted to give my dad something special that Christmas as I knew his days were numbered. I penned this song and sang it for him and my mom for a Christmas gift. We did it over Skype, and as I looked at my dad's face and sang this song, I saw tears running down his precious face, a sight I'll never forget. Now he is in his eternal home with his Savior who he deeply loved and worshipped, and he is whole again.

And now…it is well with his soul and mine.

"Heaven Is Our Home"

By Stephanie Midthun

For Dad and Mom

No more tears

There will be no more pain

No more sorrow

There will be no more shame

It's washed away, Washed away

No more sickness
There will be no more confusion
No more darkness
There will be no more sleepless nights
Only light, Holy light

(CHORUS)
Life, Forevermore
With You, our loving Father
Our minds and bodies are restored
Heaven is our home, Heaven is our home

No more strife
There will be no more heartache
No more suffering
There will be no more death
Only life, Eternal life

Weeping lasts for a night
But joy comes in the morning
Lift your eyes, Hope arise
Heaven is our home (repeat)

REFLECTION QUESTIONS

1. Are you able to grieve the losses and changes in your life in a healthy way?

2. Are you able to release outcomes to God?

3. How are you able to say "it is well with my soul"?

II.

Legacy of Life

What are you doing now that will outlast you?

What inheritance will you leave to those who come after you? What heritage will they receive? What footprint will you leave behind in each place where you live and minister?

WE THOUGHT A LOT ABOUT THE IMPORTANCE OF LEGACY WHEN Stephanie's dad passed away. We were reflecting on the legacy of his strong character and faith. His handwritten testimony from thirty years prior was found—he had placed it with his will many years earlier. It was powerful to read his own words hand-written on hotel stationary when he was away as a pilot on one of his trips. Our youngest son read it at his funeral and it was such a poignant moment. It struck us how all of us should write our story of faith for future generations to know.

For me (Joel) as a fourth-generation pastor and third-generation missionary, coming back to Africa was like a full-circle moment. In 1925, my great-grandfather, Reverend Knut Olaf Lundeberg, commissioned my grandfather, Reverend Louis Hofstad, and his daughter, Agnes (Lundeberg) Hofstad, to go to Madagascar as full-time missionaries. There my mom lived as a missionary kid and eventually as a missionary herself.

Now, living in Tanzania, I feel the momentum and favor that I have with people and organizations because of the heritage I was given. Choices that they made fifty years ago are still affecting me today. And choices that I am making will affect the lives of others many years from now.

Isn't that incredible? We have the power to affect our children, those we work with, and those we have not even met by the power of our choices—the things we decide to do and the pitfalls we avoid; whether we make sacrifices or live primarily for ourselves; whether we take risks or play it safe. Even the amount of work we do to grow our character or emotional health can mean a drastic difference for those who will come after us.

Did you know that even our failures can leave a positive legacy? Pastor Bill Johnson says that no advance in the kingdom of God is ever wasted. Whatever ground or breakthrough we have taken in the kingdom, even if it appears to have failed, is still ground that was taken for another to build on in the future. We say to our kids, "Our ceiling is your floor." Meaning that our kids get to start where we left off. Whether it is financial, education, emotional health, or spiritual authority—we are able to build on what our parents, teachers, pastors, leaders, coaches, or mentors gave us.

Americans in 2018 are obsessed with terms like equality, justice, and privilege. Those who have been given advantages due to their sex, race, education, or parent's wealth are told to "check their privilege" at the door, meaning that they should be mindful of all that was given to them that they did not earn, simply by being born in a certain place or family. For instance, if you are born in the U.S., you are automatically in the top ten percent of the wealthiest people on the planet. While it is helpful for us to be aware of our advantages and privileges, staying humble and realizing that what we accomplish is always built on those who have come before us is a good thing. It is not helpful or constructive to feel guilt or shame about it. What we have received is not up to us—but what we do with it is.

Jesus never taught about "checking your privilege," but he did teach about "using your privilege." In fact, there are many Bible verses that teach about how we receive different gifts, different amounts of resources (talents), and different levels of authority, and so on. In the parable of the talents, Jesus says that it's not about how much you have been given, but how you use it (Matt. 25:14–30). In the parable of the lamps, Jesus also states "to whom much is given, much is expected" (Luke 12:48).

This is what motivates Bill Gates and his foundation (the largest transparent private foundation in the world) that pours billions of dollars into improving healthcare, education, technology, farming, and other things in developing countries. Here is what he said in his 2007 speech at Harvard University's graduation:

My mother, who was filled with pride the day I was admitted here, never stopped pressing me to do more for others. A few days before my wedding, she hosted a bridal event, at which she read aloud a letter about marriage that she had written to Melinda. My mother was very ill with cancer at the time, but she saw one more opportunity to deliver her message, and at the close of the letter she said: "From those to whom much is given, much is expected." [10]

Whoever we are, whatever we have been given, we are leaving a legacy whether we or other people see it or not. This can be a legacy of life—one that leaves life, truth, faith, peace, confidence, and freedom to others; or a legacy of death—one that takes life and leaves confusion, anxiety, discouragement, shame, bitterness, strongholds, and chains.

We are often very aware of how much other people and life experiences have affected us, but we are often less aware of how much we have affected others. It is an amazing gift to have the potential to shape and influence those who you have never met—those coming after you. They may one day hear a story about your life, read something you wrote, or benefit from something you did.

I think about couples who came to our church on the verge of divorce, only to surrender their lives to Christ, experience healing, and build a great marriage. How will this affect their kids and grandkids? How will this affect their friends and relatives?

I think about the girls who have come to Courage House beaten, broken, and bruised, only to experience unconditional love, regular encouragement, and quality education. How will this change the generations to follow—the destiny of their children? How will this give hope to those from their villages or neighborhoods? How will this influence their friends from the past?

SONG STORY: FAITHFUL

This song was written by my youngest sister, Christy, which Threefour:one had recorded on our third album. It was the title song. Here's the story.

"Faithful" was written during a time of meditating on what God promises in His Word, to show His faithfulness and love to thousands of generations for those who love Him (Ex. 20:6; Deut. 7:9; Ps. 103:17). I reflected on how the Lord has been faithful in my own family, particularly with the legacy of faith that our parents have given us. Our family has experienced the fulfillment of promise after promise as we have dedicated our lives to Him. It has not always been easy, but through every season of life, He has shown us over and over that He is with us, that He has a plan for our family, and that He is truly faithful to fulfill His promises.

"Faithful"

By Christy Martin Eskes

Throughout the ages, a thousand generations
Your people have called You by name
Your judgments are righteous, You dwell among us
Holy God, You are the same

(CHORUS)
You are faithful to all generations
You are worthy of all our praise
You are mighty and awesome in power
You have been faithful

Throughout our lives, in the good and the hard times
You walk beside us in grace
When we are hurting, still we are learning
To cry out and seek Your face

The giver of life, Creator and friend
The Alpha, Omega, the beginning and end
A pillar of fire, a voice from on high
You opened the heavens, and You poured out Your life

REFLECTION QUESTIONS

1. What legacy have you been given?

2. What generational blessings?

3. What legacy are you hoping to give to those who come after you?

12.

Writing Your Own Song

FOR MANY YEARS, I (JOEL) PLAYED IN BUSTED FLAT, A COVER BAND IN Sacramento, CA. (It was a way for me to relax with some of my good friends and play fun music.) We played 60s/70s blues and soul music. We were a cover band, which means we covered, or played, other people's songs. We played songs from the amazing blues singer Susan Tedeschi, to the Queen of Soul Aretha Franklin, to legendary singer/ songwriter Carol King. And we were pretty good at it! But you know what, we never played our own music—we never played any songs that we wrote.

I think many of us are the same. We have gotten very good at singing other people's songs. We become experts at copying what others have done in their life, career, or ministry. Many of us are not brave enough to try singing our own songs or play our own music. We see what God is doing through this person or that ministry and we compare ourselves to it. We miss out on the new and original thing God wants to do through us because of comparison. When we compare with others it leads to one of two bad places: either we become proud and feel better than others, or we become discouraged and feel less than others.

But God has a new song for us to sing—one that He composes throughout our lives. In Ephesians 2:10, God calls us his workmanship, "For we are God's workmanship, created in Christ Jesus to do good works, which God prepared in advance for us to do."

The word used for workmanship is the Greek word *poiema*; it is the same word that we get the English word "poem" from. We are literally God's poem—the ultimate artistic expression of God's creativity. There is no being more creative than God and we are the pinnacle of His work.

Hebrews 12:1 says: *Therefore, since we are surrounded by such a great cloud of witnesses, let us throw off everything that hinders and the sin that so easily entangles, and let us run with perseverance the race marked out for us.*

Some of the keys to finishing well are stated here; first, realize that many have finished the race before you—it is possible! Second, travel light—what do you need to say "no" to so that you can say "yes" to Jesus? Third, run with perseverance or steadfast endurance—this is not a patience that just accepts things the way they are, but a patience that masters those things through unhurried determination.[11]

Run the Race Marked Out for You

You will not be successful running the wrong race, or the race that is meant for someone else to run.

We have worked with many different churches, denominations, non-profit organizations, and business leaders to fight the evil of human sex trafficking of children. We have found that in this one issue almost every human on the planet agrees: it is wrong for children to be sold for sex! The truth is, we all have a role to play in this battle. In other words, we all have a place on the wall. We can be working in the legal realm or prevention or running a home for victims or organizing a race to raise funds. All the roles are different, but they are all necessary and equally important. Jenny Williamson says it this way, "Do what you love to do—but do it for these kids—bake, run, paint, play music, write; but do it with a purpose."

We have a Lutheran heritage, a Spirit-filled experience, and an evangelical heart. I belong to a healthy network of churches called the ARC (Alliance of Renewal Churches). We seek to take the best of sacramental, evangelical, and charismatic theology because we believe that each one reveals and emphasizes a different part of God's heart. We value relationship (love) as much as we value doctrine (truth) and we live in the tension of not compromising either of them.

The Lutheran church that we planted and led for eighteen years (Living Water Church) was a hybrid—we had a niche in our community as a church that had communion every week, biblical expository preaching, spirit-led modern worship music, and regular opportunity for healing/prophetic prayer. We had to learn to find our "own sound"—our church was different than most and my laid-back leadership style was also different than most, but God used it. We had our place on the wall.

Each believer and leader have a place on the wall in the kingdom of God—this is called having a kingdom mentality. Each healthy, life-giving church has an important place in the body of Christ. Some of us were created to pastor smaller churches, some are wired for large churches, some for more traditional expressions, and some for more modern ones. We are from different tribes, but we are all Israelites who fight a common enemy to enter a shared promised land. I'll never forget Francis Frangipane reminding a group of us pastors and leaders, "Jesus is coming back for a bride, not a harem!"

Finding your own sound doesn't mean you have to start from scratch—others can teach and influence you—but at some point, you need to find your own sound. Name any popular band from the Beatles to U2 to Coldplay. The Beatles were influenced by Chuck Berry; U2 was influenced by the Beatles; and Coldplay was influenced by U2. They each took something old and made it different—expressing it in a new way.

As our church got more involved in ministry to the "least of these," some took this to a new level. Our first response as a church was to use concerts to raise funds to help street children in Africa. But as the years went on, many in our church expressed this same heart for the least of these in different ways. Some families adopted children internationally and domestically. Many went through the volunteer training and became involved in fighting human trafficking and mentoring the girls at Courage House. Still others championed new ways to help at-risk parents and their kids stay together through temporary foster care, and a few began regularly ministering to the homeless in our city. The point is, each took their passion and ran with it in a new direction—one that God was calling them to, and the kingdom grew!

Now we live in Africa, and we are still doing hybrid ministry. We are overseeing Courage House and its expansion, fighting sex trafficking at many levels, and ministering to leaders, missionaries, and pastors from many denominations for emotional health. Has anyone done that before? It doesn't matter—it only matters that God has called us to do this for now. He has taken all we have learned and the good things that others have poured into us, as well as our own weaknesses and mistakes, and is doing something new through it all.

Two of our personal heroes we've mentioned in this book are Jenny Williamson and Darla Calhoun. Both women are strong pioneers and said yes to God's call. Both have impacted their communities and Africa, and they have made a massive difference in the lives of children who are victims of the streets—and sex trafficking. Jenny started Courage Houses in California and Tanzania, and Darla started Agape Children's Ministry for street children in Kenya and it is expanding. These women know about perseverance. They both have found their own sound and place on the wall, and because of that, God has changed the lives of hundreds, even thousands, of children who would otherwise be addicted, homeless, hopeless, or even dead. Because of them, captives are being set free and generations are being changed forever!

When you find your own sound and write your own song, just watch what God will do! He has something beautiful to accomplish in you and through you, and if you don't do it, the song may never be heard and lives may never be changed!

Song Story: You Are Able/Unaweza

We met these four older boys at Agape Children's Ministry in Kenya in 2003. These boys were the first ones who Mama Darla brought into her home and offered a safe place, told them of God's love, and gave them a chance at a new life. These boys loved to sing and worship and even wrote some beautiful, original worship songs. This simple song, "You Are Able" (Unaweza), touched our hearts, and they sang it with such beautiful harmonies. We had to capture it on the He Knows My Name CD, and we still sing it today!

"You Are Able/Unaweza"

By the Agape Boys
(SHADRACK, KISALA, ISAIAH, AND CALVIN)

You are able, Jesus You are able
You are able, Jesus You are able
I give all the glory to You Lord Jesus

You are able
I give all the glory to You Lord Jesus
You are able

Unaweza, Bwana unaweza
Unaweza, Bwana unaweza
Tua kupa utukufu na sifa Bwana
Unaweza
Tua kupa utukufu na sifa Bwana
Unaweza

REFLECTION QUESTIONS

1. What is your song, your sound, your passion? Reflect on Ephesians 2:10. What kind of poem did God write when He created you?

2. What makes you glad? Sad? Mad? Reflect on Hebrews 12:1. Are you running the race God marked out for you, or are you trying to run someone else's race?

3. Who are the three to four people or ministries that have influenced you or inspired you the most? Write them a note to tell them!

4. Is God speaking to you now? Take time to listen to His voice and allow Him to creatively use you for His kingdom purposes! Unaweza! (You are able!)

13.

Finishing Well

"He must increase, but I must decrease." (John 3:30)

JOHN THE BAPTIST KNEW WHEN TO LET GO. IT IS HUMAN NATURE TO HANG on. Sports stars always play one season too long; people in power always fight even when the battle is over; and pastors are notorious for sabotaging their successor. In Africa where power is king, Julius Nyerere, who became the first president of Tanzania in 1964, is the only modern African leader who was not forced to resign presidential power. He voluntarily did this in 1985 when he realized that the country needed new leadership and direction.

There are times and seasons in each of our lives when it is time to let go, time to move on, time to let the next person have an opportunity. Just as it says in Ecclesiastes 3:1–2,

There is a time for everything, and a season for every activity under heaven: a time to be born and a time to die, a time to plant and a time to uproot.

This hit me one day as I was reading and praying about God's direction for us. "A time to plant, and a time to uproot..." We had planted, but now it was time to uproot, time to change, time to leave everything we knew, and all the relationships we had developed. Oh, how I wanted to stay—to coast and enjoy what we had built and prepared for retirement. Uprooting doesn't sound fun, and it isn't, but it is necessary if God is leading.

"Everything you want is just outside your comfort zone."
~ Pastor John Bullock

These words in a sermon rang true as I sat with twenty others in a makeshift living room, six-month-old church plant in Moshi, Tanzania led by our new U.K. friends.

EVERYTHING YOU WANT?

Eight months prior, we had realized God was calling us to go to Tanzania full time. Our motto at Living Water Church was "Glorify, Grow, and Go." As many families came and went or moved away for jobs or other reasons, we often joked that we needed to change our motto to "Glorify, Grow, and STAY a while." Change and distance is painful but necessary sometimes. As my good friend Pastor Nathan Hoff says, "everyone wants to see God move, but nobody wants to move!"

Yet God was calling us to go. I remember praying one night over this huge potential transition. I was asking God all the usual questions: *What about the church? What about our sons? What about my retirement...?* After I was ready to listen, He said one thing:

> *"Just wait and see what I am going to do; it will be better than you can imagine."*

That was enough—it was all I needed to hear. The rest was just a decision to believe and trust in Him or not.

God knows what we think we want—and He knows what we really want deep inside even when we don't. And He knows that it is waiting for us—just outside our comfort zone.

And now as we write this book on a couch in Africa, we can say that it is better than we ever imagined and we are more fulfilled than we ever thought we could be.

CHIEF SERVANT

On my last Sunday at Living Water, I held in my hand a Maasai chief's club that I had bought on our first trip to Kenya in 2003. A long-time resident in my office, it represented leadership and authority. As I thought about our church transitioning from eighteen years of my leadership to my associate, Rob Lane, who the church was calling to be the new Senior Pastor, I knew this was what I was to give him. Although it signified authority, I knew that Rob's and my thoughts on authority were the same. I had seen Rob's heart for people and that he was a servant leader. I had seen him vacuum, clean toilets, and take out the garbage. He served the church while Stephanie and I were away in Africa for a three-month mission trip and sabbatical. I had heard about his handling of difficult situations with humility and strength, his protecting the unity of the church, and honoring our leadership in every way—he did a great job. We had heard African pastors joke about how, if they ever left their church for that long, it would no longer be theirs when they returned!

Jesus said, "But among you it will be different. Whoever wants to be a leader among you must be your servant" (Matt. 20:26, NLT).

So, as I handed over the Maasai chief's club to him as my last act as Senior Pastor, I said the words, "Now you are the Chief Servant."

As I did this, we embraced, and I wept as I felt the overwhelming deep emotions of eighteen years of love, pain, highs, lows, relationships, friendships, healings, conflicts, and responsibility leave my body—and I felt the emotions of our church and their acceptance over Rob's new role.

They had seen his heart too.

FINISHING WELL

One thing we can be sure of in life is that there will be change. Transitions are not an option—they will happen. But you do have a choice in how they happen. You do have a choice in how you respond to it. You can choose to finish well.

But we are all human. As the date for us to leave Living Water grew closer, I felt the urge to continue to control certain decisions and influence how the church would move forward. The tension of letting go after being in charge for many years grew stronger and I felt the stress in my thoughts, emotions, and body. Resisting the temptation to hold on to what was and let others take the ship in another direction was exhausting me. One day, Stephanie had finally had enough and said, "You need to let go of Living Water." Sigh. She was right, and by the grace of God, I did. And the transition ended being very healthy as I began to step back and Rob stepped up.

Our friend and president of the ARC, Mike Bradley, came to commission us to go to Africa and commission Rob as Senior Pastor on our last Sunday. He remarked that in thirty years of church leadership experience, he's never seen such a healthy transition of leadership as he saw at Living Water.

The truth is that how we finish at one season is often how we will start another. We need to have a good ending to have a good beginning. We have seen so many people end badly, whether leaving a church, a marriage, a job, or a ministry position. When a person does not end well, it can affect the next season adversely. That same person most likely will not be content in the next church, marriage, or job.

When you bless and honor your successor, you are blessed. When you voluntarily let God "decrease" you in one area, it allows Him to "increase" you in another. One season of ministry must die in peace for another season to be born healthy.

What are some unhealthy ways to finish? One way is to sabotage your exit by blaming others, which does not allow them or you to move on in peace. Another way people finish poorly is by giving in to the temptation to put down their former church, former spouse, or former boss. But this critical attitude ends by polluting any future opportunity or relationship.

Thinking back to the trauma-drama triangle, there are three toxic roles that we tend to fall into during times of stress: rescuer, persecutor, and victim. When we are in transition we can go into persecutor mode—trying to control and manipulate people and outcomes. We can go into victim mode—giving up and being passive. We can also go into rescuer mode—helping and enabling others to soothe and distract from our own pain and anxiety.

Letting go is what releases us into the next season and the next breakthrough. Hebrews 11:17–19 says,

> "By faith Abraham, when God tested him, offered Isaac as a sacrifice. He who had received the promises was about to sacrifice his one and only son, even though God had said to him, "It is through Isaac that your offspring will be reckoned." Abraham reasoned that God could raise the dead, and figuratively speaking, he did receive Isaac back from death."

What is the ultimate test of letting go? Giving up your son, not only your only child, but the symbol of *all* the promises God has given you for the future. But to Abraham, this was a rational decision; "Abraham reasoned that God could raise the dead." If God is really God, it is rational to believe He can raise the dead, that He can birth something new, and that a breakthrough can come—if we will only let go.

I (Stephanie) just ended a phone call with Jenny Williamson as Courage Worldwide is going through a transition in California. We were reflecting on the past several years of our work with the many children who are victims of sex trafficking. It was an incredible journey with twists and turns that were so very exciting and so very exhausting. We saw the dream unfold as Courage House opened and as the community wrapped their arms around the organization. We saw dozens of girls' lives change—girls who came with no hope and then who blossomed into beautiful, smart, and strong young women, all because they were given a home and a family. We were reflecting on all that God had done these last nine years since the day I met Jenny. And now it's a new season.

California has changed its laws regarding caring for minor children, and long-term group homes are no longer allowed. Courage House is a long-term group home, and with our program we had very good and successful outcomes for over five years since opening in 2011. In fact, with the proven results, our outcomes were some of the best in the nation, we were told by leading experts. California changed the law to require children who are victims of trafficking to go to a short-term mental health treatment facility for six months and then transition to a resource family (foster home). We think this is a huge mistake as we've learned that the girls need more time to heal as most of them won't be ready for a family and/or most families are not prepared to deal with their level of trauma. It's a 24/7 effort and takes a team of trained professionals to help our girls. Families are simply not equipped—no matter how good they are or how well they love. We learned this the hard way.

Besides, foster care has not worked in the past with our girls—and it's not like families are lining up to take in highly traumatized teenage girls. After much prayer, Courage Worldwide in California is focusing on working with over 18-year-olds who are victims of trafficking. We trust that God will continue His work in setting captives free and we know that all the years of experience with minors will bear fruit. More than fifty people in different states and countries are asking for help in opening a Courage House for minors, and the prototype is nearly finished. It's a new chapter with new freedom to expand.

Letting go was not easy until God spoke very clearly to Jenny's heart. I'll never forget a few months ago when Jenny was preaching in Southern California at Trinity Lutheran Church in San Pedro after we had done a Courage Conference the previous day. She felt that the Lord gave her a message on "pruning" for this newer partner church and she wasn't sure why. I was leading worship and when we finished worshipping, Jenny began to speak and she was very emotional. She wanted to share with this church—this generous group of believers, who were the ones to recently purchase our property in Tanzania. She said through tears, "Well church, I prepared a message for you on 'pruning' but the Lord told me during worship today that it was a message for me." Up to that point, she wasn't ready to let go of the Northern CA property and the fight to be able to continue to work with minors. But during worship, Jenny heard God's voice clearly that it was time to *let go*. It was a defining moment for her and the organization. I always respected Jenny's obedience to the Lord and trusting Him for the next season.

It was a joy to host Jenny in Tanzania recently to meet all our new girls and their babies, encourage our staff and board, and process what God is doing in the expansion here. She was able to see that her dream is being fulfilled; girls who suffered greatly now have a good home and family, are on their healing journey, they know their purpose, and are getting a good education. Some of our girls are in college now, some are in their careers, and some are married with children. We had dinner with the Archbishop and Assistant Bishop of the Evangelical Lutheran Church of Tanzania and their wives. They have hearts to see more captives free and join us in this fight. Before Jenny left, we had a baptism of eight of our girls and two of them dedicated their young sons to the Lord. God is moving powerfully to bring freedom—what a joy to be a part of what He is doing!

I, Stephanie, had another dream soon after we moved to Tanzania that seemed very significant to us and to Courage Worldwide. I don't think I'll ever forget it, just like the dream I told you about in the beginning of this book that I had over thirty years ago.

This dream was also about worship.

In my dream, I wanted to get together for dinner and a time of worship with our good friends in a partner organization based in Sacramento that also fights trafficking. They said to me, "Stephanie, this time let us lead worship." So they did. I sat in the front row with a group of young Cambodian children as they got on stage and I noticed that Jenny was in the back of the room. The team began to sing and the music was so beautiful—it carried me away in glorious worship and I didn't want it to end. When the music stopped, a woman stepped up to the microphone and looked at me and with a voice of authority said, *"The bullet in your chest is now removed."* I felt something physically shift in my spirit and looked back at Jenny and we knew this was a word for us and for Courage Worldwide. I woke up the next morning and emailed Jenny about my dream, and as she was reading my email, she said she also felt a shift in her spirit. The enemy had been trying to discourage us and make us quit and now we felt like we could breathe again. This was a defining moment where we knew that God was saying that there is now a new season with new life and growth and for us to move forward with great expectation.

So, we open our hearts and our hands, laying everything on the altar, surrendering it all to our Father, knowing that He is good. Knowing that He has a plan. His purposes will prevail and He is with us and will complete all that He has begun. He is the one who sets the captive free. He is the one who has set us free!

To God be *all* the glory.

SONG STORY: ABBA FATHER (MY VERY FIRST SONG)

My two sisters and I recorded our first acoustic album *Heart of Worship* in 1999. Both are songwriters and contributed a few original songs to that album. Songwriting wasn't my gifting—I loved to direct choirs, lead worship, and lead music ministry. Our friend Marv Quam, who had a strong prophetic gift, told me soon after that recording that the Lord told him I would be writing songs and that we sisters would be recording five albums. I told Marv it wasn't my gift and he said to me, "Just watch what the Lord will do." I had forgotten about that conversation, but a couple of months later I was at a conference when out of nowhere I started hearing a song in my head. I couldn't shake it and started singing the melody and had to leave the room for a bit to put it all on paper. This was my first original song. Thank you, dear Marv (who is now in heaven), for encouraging me even though I doubted you, and myself. Expressing my heart through music, using it to help others, and learning to fight battles through worship has forever changed my life. And thank you, my Abba Father—my gentle Shepherd—for setting me free and saving my life. I trust You to lead us and we will follow.

"Abba Father"

By Stephanie Midthun

Where can I go, where do I turn
But to You, my Lord
I lift my eyes and raise my hands
To Your throne I surrender

Oh Lord Your presence stirs my soul
Your joy gives me strength wherever I go
My hope is in You, for You've chosen me as Your own
I am Your child, Abba Father
Your voice so still, leads me on
It's Your will, Oh Lord
I'll take my cross and follow You
Where You lead, Abba Father

I was lost now am found
Was bound now I'm free
To be Your child and serve You Lord
For all eternity

REFLECTION QUESTIONS

1. Are you in a season of transition? How have you handled transition in the past? Do you tend to go into "persecutor-control" mode or "victim-passive" mode?

2. Is God calling you to let go of anything right now? Reflect on Hebrews 11:17.

3. Ask God to help you embrace the new seasons He has for you. Read John 3:30. Is God calling you to decrease in some way so that someone else can increase?

Father, give us strength to endure and align us,
Oh Lord, with Your heart and Your purposes.
Let us know when our season is done. Show us Your
way and Your perfect timing. We know that Your
thoughts are higher than our thoughts and Your ways
are higher than ours too. Help us to let go when it's
hard and trust You completely in the transition that
we are in for the new season that You have for us.

We confess that it is not easy. Help us to end well
and to bless and honor those we've worked with
or worked for—even if it's been a challenge. Help
us to move on in life and health and with great
expectation for the new season that is ahead.

We trust You to lead us, to equip us, and to
strengthen us when the battle rages around us.
We trust You with all that we are leaving behind, and
we believe in Your promises for what lies ahead!

You are good!

Thank you, Jesus, for setting our hearts free,
so that we can bring freedom to others! Thank
you for making beauty out of ashes! And thank
you that we can display Your splendor as You
complete the beautiful work you've begun.

In Your Holy Name,

Amen

✛ FINAL THOUGHTS ✛

ALTHOUGH SHE CAN BE A SHY LADY, I AM USUALLY ABLE TO CATCH A clear glimpse of her in the mornings and early evenings. She shines in the sunlight and broods at night. She changes atmospheres around her and affects the climate. From her flows life in the form of clouds, rain, and rivers. Her beauty is unmatched—breathtaking waterfalls, vibrant flowers, and lush forests are all around her. She grows healthy fruit and rich coffee. Although she is challenging, thousands come to see her from all over the world every year.

As you may have guessed by now, I am not speaking about my wife (another beautiful creation of God) but about Mount Kilimanjaro—the "rooftop of Africa" that we can see here in Moshi every day. In fact, the reason that the town of Moshi exists is because of the mountain. The highest peak on Kilimanjaro is called "Uhuru" or "Freedom." Every day it calls out to us that freedom is visible and possible, but it is not easy. Every year over 35,000 people attempt to make the five- to eight-day climb, spending around $2,500 for the "privilege" and pain of trying. For the eight out of ten people who summit the mountain, they have some things in common.

Each person who reaches the top had to push through when they thought they couldn't go any further. Freedom is work. But freedom is worth it. Fighting for your own healing or fighting for others takes great courage and perseverance through the momentary setbacks and battles that come against us and wear us out.

Mount Kilimanjaro is over 19,000 feet tall and to successfully reach the top, "Uhuru (Freedom) Peak," the key is to adjust slowly to the thin air. As we ascend to new levels and higher places in our lives, there is nothing better than standing on the mountains we've conquered and looking back at the breakthroughs God brought us through and how even the battles made us stronger. But it is usually not a quick process. It's sweet victory over the powers of darkness that have tried to take us out of our calling, and it gives us confidence to move forward in our race and to cheer others on as well!

There is a great cloud of witnesses in heaven cheering us all on. We can picture our dads and family waving and clapping, celebrating our growth and perseverance.

And, we are cheering you on too!

The world is waiting for you to live out your freedom song. Captives are waiting to be free and there is nothing better than joining Jesus in changing their stories. You will display his splendor as you allow him to do what he does best in your life and through your life, making beauty out of the ashes—it gives God glory!

This is the courageous adventure of freedom where God invites each of us to join Him. A journey of doubts and faith, fear and love, pain and joy, suffering and healing, shame and grace, work and rest, planting and uprooting—battles and breakthroughs.

✣ NOTES ✣

(1)   Warner, Marcus. *What Every Believer Should Know About...Spiritual Warfare.* (Deeper Walk International, 2015).

(2)   Groves, Shaun. "Worship and Missions." Worship Leader Magazine, August, 2003.

(3)   Haugen, Gary. *Just Courage.* (Downers Grove: InterVaristy Press, 2009).

(4)   Emerald, David. *The Power of TED: The Empowerment Dynamic.* (Bainbridge Island: Polaris Publishing, 2010).

(5)   Scazerro, Peter. *Emotionally Healthy Spirituality.* (Grand Rapids: Zondervan, 2017).

(6)   Walter, Robert. *If I'm Forgiven, Why Do I Feel so Bad?* 2016.

(7)   Scazerro, Peter. *Emotionally Healthy Spirituality.* (Grand Rapids: Zondervan, 2017).

(8)   Warren, Rick. The Purpose Driven Life. (Grand Rapids: Zondervan, 2013). (Day 19)

(9)   http://www.staugustine.com/living/religion/2014-10-16/story-behind-song-it-well-my-soul

(10)   Gates, Bill. "Remarks of Bill Gates" Harvard Commencement 2007. https://news.harvard.edu/gazette/story/2007/06/remarks-of-bill-gates-harvard-commencement-2007/

(11)   Barclay, William. *Daily Study Bible.* https://www.studylight.org/commentaries/dsb/hebrews-12.html

(12)   U.S. Department of State. "Trafficking in Persons Report 2018." https://www.state.gov/j/tip/rls/tiprpt/2018/

* ABOUT THE AUTHORS *

⧼◦⧽

Pastor Joel and Stephanie Midthun have worked in full-time ministry for more than thirty years in the Lutheran Church. After working for ten years on staff at Trinity Lutheran (Norwalk, CA) and three years as an associate pastor at St. Peter's Lutheran (Elk Grove, CA), Joel and a team from St. Peter's planted Living Water Church in Elk Grove, California, where he was the senior pastor for eighteen years. Stephanie was a music director and worship leader in the churches where Joel pastored and is also a singer and songwriter. She recorded several albums with her sisters (their name "Threefour:one" is based on Psalm 34:1).

Joel and Stephanie have been involved with ministry to street children in Kenya as well as fighting sex trafficking with Courage Worldwide, both in the U.S. and in Africa. Stephanie launched benefit CD's and concerts to bring awareness to the community on the plight of street children and trafficking victims. In 2017, Joel and Stephanie moved to Tanzania, Africa full time, and it felt like going "home," as Joel was born in Madagascar and grew up as a missionary kid there. They now oversee Courage House Tanzania—a home for children who are victims of human sex trafficking and its expansion in Africa under Courage Worldwide, Inc.

Pastor Joel and Stephanie also do trainings and seminars on human trafficking, emotional health, and more, and they love working with and equipping pastors, leaders, and missionaries in Africa and the U.S. Currently they are partnering with one of the largest Lutheran bodies in the world in Tanzania—the ELCT (Evangelical Lutheran Church of Tanzania), that is committed to leading the church in fighting trafficking and providing homes for its young victims in Tanzania. Joel and Stephanie have three grown sons and enjoy hiking, swimming, music, traveling, and spending time with their beloved family.

To contact Joel and Stephanie, you may email them at revmidthun@gmail.com or s.midthun@courageworldwide.org. You can follow their journey on Facebook @joelandstephmidthun.

Some of the songs mentioned in this book are available on iTunes and proceeds support Courage Worldwide. You can find the Believe in Me and Come Back Home albums by Courage Worldwide there. The other songs by Stephanie and her sisters (threefour:one) are available on CD. You can contact us for more information.

✤ ABOUT OUR MISSION ✤

Courage Worldwide Tanzania

Contact Information
Pastor Joel & Stephanie Midthun

U.S. mailing address:
3031 Stanford Ranch Rd. #339, Suite 2, Rocklin, CA 95765

Tanzania mailing address:
P.O. Box 8161 Moshi, Tanzania
Email: revmidthun@gmail.com; s.midthun@courageworldwide.org
Facebook: @joelandstephmidthun

Courage Worldwide
www.courageworldwide.org
3031 Stanford Ranch Rd. #339, Suite 2, Rocklin, CA 95765
916.685.6161
info@courageworldwide.org

General Information

We are Executive Directors of Courage House in Moshi, Tanzania—a home and school for victims of human (sex) trafficking under the age of 18. We also oversee Courage House Too—a transition home for girls over 18 years old, opening January 2019. We are expanding and will have forty-five beds between the two homes, and by 2020 we will have seventy beds when the build-out of our property is complete. In 2018, we launched our C2BU—

Courage to Be You School, which is Form 2 and Form 4 high school for the girls at Courage House, and a preschool for their children and staff children (3–5 years old).

We also provide training to pastors, leaders, students, and young adults on the topics of human trafficking, the effects of trauma, emotional health, and more. We are partnering with the Evangelical Lutheran Church in Tanzania–Northern Diocese to train their leaders and pastors and work together to prevent trafficking, locate victims, and start more Courage Houses in Tanzania for victims of trafficking. We also partner with many other denominations and have done trainings with pastors and leaders as well. We work with government and are launching a Human Trafficking Task Force in the Kilimanjaro region. Our hope is to expand it to all of Tanzania as well as other countries in Africa under Courage Worldwide's "Not in My Country" campaign. This campaign has been successful in the U.S. as the Not in My City, Not in My State campaign. It has brought different sectors together in various cities to fight trafficking. No child should be sold for sex for any reason. It's our heart's cry to help stop this growing evil against children—both girls and boys—and to give them a place to heal and be restored.

Courage House Tanzania Expansion

We have a vision in the next five years to open Courage Houses in three other regions in Tanzania as God provides the resources. Because of the many requests from other African countries, our hope is to expand beyond Tanzania in the next five years.

Courage House Global Expansion (Prototype)

The big and bold vision of Courage Worldwide is to build a home in every city that needs one. Because of the excellent outcomes of Courage Worldwide with our first two long-term pilot homes for victims of sex trafficking in California and Tanzania, people from many different countries are asking for help. We believe this vision comes from God and can only be accomplished by Him! So far, over fifty people have asked for the prototype of Courage House from around the world and many have gone through the certified training as a start. At this time (2018), the needed materials for the prototype are nearly finished. Contact Courage Worldwide about bringing a home to your region by emailing info@ courageworldwide.org.

Funding and Financial Accountability

Information on finances can be found at www.courageworldwide.org. 990 forms are available on the website and financials can be requested. CWW is currently in good standing with the ECFA, Charity Navigator, and GuideStar.

How to Give

Send checks to:

Courage Worldwide (write Tanzania in the memo)

3031 Stanford Ranch Rd. #339, Suite 2, Rocklin, CA 95765

You can also pay online at www.courageworldwide.org/donate (put "Tanzania" in the "notes" section if you want to designate for Tanzania).

Individual and Church Partner Involvement

First, we need ongoing prayer support—the battle against human trafficking is often closely connected to hideous evil and tremendous spiritual warfare.

Second, regular commitment to our general fund will help create a strong financial foundation to build from. Individual, corporate, and church donors are welcome—every dollar given matters!

Third, we encourage pastors, leaders, and anyone who wants to help to come to Tanzania and bring volunteers. Contact us if you are interested in partnering with us.

Sex Trafficking Statistics

Per the United States government and the United Nations, the selling of individuals is both a global and local problem translating to billions of dollars and millions of victims. In the U.S. alone, it is estimated there are hundreds of thousands of at-risk youth who are vulnerable to this type of commercial sexual exploitation. In the locations where we have residential homes—California and Tanzania—we have received well over four hundred calls for placement for children as young as eight years old. It is our passion at Courage Worldwide to collect data on the girls that we serve so that we can report our outcomes—both our successes and our challenges.

According to the Global Trafficking in Persons Report 2018,[12] human trafficking is one of the fastest growing crimes in the world. The trafficking of humans splinters families, distorts global markets, encourages other criminal activities, costs the country millions of dollars, and threatens public safety and national security. However, the greatest consequence of this crime is that it robs individuals of their freedom and dignity. That's why we as a community, along with our government leaders, must join the global movement to pursue an end to the scourge of human trafficking in our country and around the world and provide resources for its vulnerable victims. Won't you join us?

✣ RECOMMENDED RESOURCES ✣

⟡

BOOKS

Do You Have the Courage to Be You by Jenny Williamson

Uniquely You: A Faith Driven Journey to Your True Identity and Your Water-walking, Giant-slaying, History-making Destiny Bible Study Workbook by Jenny Williamson

Being a Safe Place for the Dangerous Kind by Mike Bradley

Emotionally Healthy Spirituality by Pete Scazerro

The Power of TED, "The Empowerment Dynamic" by David Emerald

Agape's Children by Darla Calhoun

Just Courage by Gary Haugen

WEBSITES

Courage Worldwide, www.courageworldwide.org

Jenny Williamson, www.jennytwilliamson.com

Agape Children's Ministry, www.agapechildren.org

Mayaba S. Choongo, www.mayabachoongo.org

Runnin' for Rhett, www.runninforrhett.org

Compassion International, www.compassioninternational.org

Holt International, www.holtinternational.org

International Justice Mission, www.ijm.org

ARC, www.allianceofrenewalchurches.org

Empowerment Dynamic, www.powerofted.com

Dr. Joe Johnson, Heart of the Father Ministry, pastorjoejohnson@gmail.com

Robert Walter (teachings on shame), www.ongodstrail.com

Information on shame, www.shamehonor.com

Dr. Gil Stieglitz, Principles to Live By, www.ptlb.com

Emotional Health and test, www.emotionallyhealthy.org

Pastor John and Debbie Bullock, www.soulcamp.org

Arise! Women, Denise Siemens, www.arisewomen.org